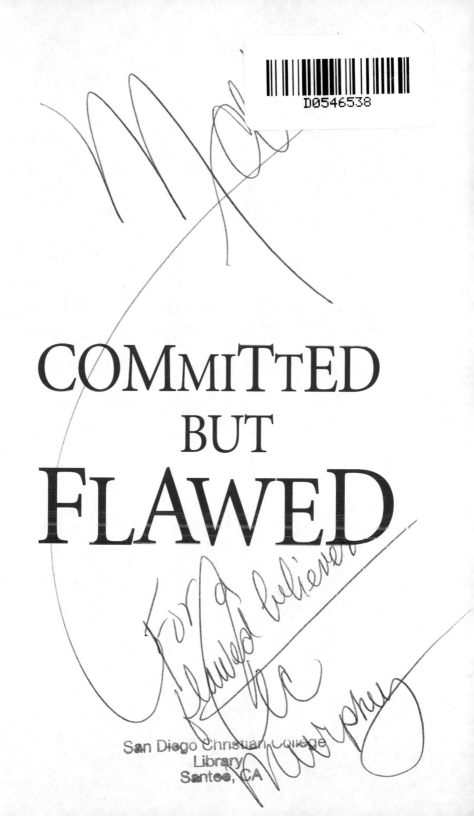

COMMITTED
BUT
FLAWED

For a flawed believer

CECIL MURPHEY

COMMITTED
BUT
FLAWED

Committed but Flawed

Copyright © 2004 by Cecil Murphey
Published by Living Ink Books, an imprint of AMG Publishers
6815 Shallowford Rd.
Chattanooga, Tennessee 37421

Translations used:
Contemporary English Version (CEV)
New International Version (NIV)
New King James Version (NKJV)
New Living Translation (NLT)
New Revised Standard Version (NRSV)
Today's New International Version (TNIV)

ISBN 0-89957-378-9

First printing—July 2004

Cover design by ImageWright, Inc., Chattanooga, Tennessee
Interior design and typesetting by Pro Production, Nanuet, New York
Edited and proofread by Eric Stanford of Stanford Creative Services, Dan Penwell,
    Bob Land of Land on Demand, and Warren Baker

Printed in the United States of America
10 09 08 07 06 05 04 –B– 8 7 6 5 4 3 2 1

CONTENTS

ACKNOWLEDGMENTS

Many people shape our lives and encourage us on our journey. I find it impossible to mention them all, but I especially want to thank the following:

Members of the Bible Discovery Sunday School class: For our decade together, I'll bet you thought I did all the teaching. You've also taught me, loved me, and forgiven my shortcomings. Thank you.

My agent Deidre Knight and her husband Jud: When I first mentioned the idea of this book, I expected both of you to tell me to forget it and focus on something else. Instead, you enthusiastically encouraged me.

Dan Penwell: You were not only one of the first editors to read my manuscript, but the first to contact my agent and make an offer. Thank you.

David Morgan: As I've told you already, "Because of you, I'm a better Christian."

Most of all, I'm grateful for my wife Shirley: I live with you and I can still say, "You're the most sincere Christian I know."

INTRODUCTION

I yearn for more of God in my life.

Through the years since my conversion, I've read the right books, heard excellent sermons, gone to in-depth seminars, and practiced what the experts told me. I learned and I grew. I still hungered for more of God.

I set up daily prayer times and faithfully read my Bible. I did all the things the spiritual giants suggested. Yet the hunger persisted.

It's not the kind of burning desire that's there every minute. At times it's stronger than at others, but the yearning lingers. That craving brought me to God as a young adult. That same desire has gnawed at me through the intervening years. "There must be more," I kept hearing myself say. I didn't even know what I meant by "more," but I yearned for a deeper, more intimate relationship with God.

After a number of years as a serious Christian, I stopped moaning that I could find no satisfaction for the hunger. Instead, I grasped that intense longing as God's way of pushing me forward—to make me grow and want to continue growing.

I also realized something else: I had to find my own way. I haven't left the tried-and-true methods of those who have walked in front of me, but I have searched for other ways to make my commitment to God more meaningful to me.

Three years ago I stopped praying the way the spiritual giants of the past urged. I didn't think they were wrong. On the contrary, their methods worked *for them*. The methods just didn't do much for my spiritual growth or unrelenting passion. So I began my own pursuit.

I also realized that many of those advocates were contemplatives—people who spent hours in prayer (or so they implied) and seemed able to read and meditate on the Bible at length each day.

I've been trying to find my own way to intensify my relationship with my Savior and friend. My methods are probably a bit unorthodox, but I don't worry about that. My goal is communion with Jesus Christ on the most intimate level I'm capable of achieving.

In the following chapters I want to share one phase of my spiritual pilgrimage. This is a method that works for me. Perhaps it will work for you, too. It is a method that focuses only on my search for a more intimate relationship with Jesus Christ; consequently, I don't discuss interceding for others, which is a part of serious prayer.

I stumbled onto a method of prayer that has enriched my spiritual relationship. Before I explain this method, though, I want to retell you a story called "The Great Stone Face." Nathaniel Hawthorne wrote it in the nineteenth century.

⇝

Young Ernest and his mother sat outside their cottage and stared at one particular New Hampshire mountain. From where they sat, they could see the outline of a great stone face carved by nature.

While they stared at the magnificent structure, Ernest's mother told him the ancient prophecy handed down from the days of the Native Americans. The legend promised that a child born in the area would become the kindest and wisest person of his time. People would recognize him because his face would bear an exact resemblance to the Great Stone Face.

"I do hope that I shall live to see him," cried Ernest.

For long periods every day, the boy stared at the Great Stone Face and felt as if the rock structure gazed back at him with great tenderness.

As Ernest matured, he waited for the wise and loving emissary to appear. Each day the boy gazed longingly at the mountain and thought of the greatness of that person who would come. In the shadow of the Great Stone Face, he studied, prayed, and meditated.

During the years he waited, he became a preacher, known widely for his compassion and wisdom. His greatest passion, however, was to meet the man who embodied the image of the Great Stone Face. He waited all through his life, and no such person appeared.

One day when Ernest was an old man, he spoke to a large crowd in a meadow with the Great Stone Face in the background. He spoke words of great depth that harmonized with the holy love and good deeds of the man's life.

One of the listeners stared at the speaker and then at the mountain. "Do you not see it?" he cried out. "Ernest is himself the likeness of the Great Stone Face!"

No one had ever noticed the resemblance before, but as they compared the visage of Ernest with the Great Stone Face, they agreed. He was the one who had been prophesied about.

By gazing at the mountain every day of his life, Ernest sought for the attributes he desired—qualities he projected on the rock structure. As he sought those qualities, they gradually developed in him. The story ends sadly, though, because Ernest never acknowledged that he had become the kind of person he had sought all his life.

〰

For me, Hawthorne's story suggests two principles.

1. We become what we focus on. Whatever we give ourselves to shapes our attitudes and determines our character. The music we listen to and the books we read do more than entertain or give us information. They actually mold our attitude and our outlook.

A couple of years ago, I began playing *America's 25 Favorite Praise & Worship Choruses* on the CD player at my desk. We rarely sing that kind of music in our church, and I don't consciously listen to the CD when it's playing. It's background to push away distractions from the noises outside on our street. Yet, recently when I was weeding my garden, I began singing—which I do a lot. The difference, however, was the realization that I had absorbed several of those praise choruses. I didn't have every word implanted in my memory, but the melody lingers there, along with most of the words. All of that came out of unconscious attention. How many of the songs would I have absorbed if I had made a conscious effort to do so?

2. Even though they may already be present, we don't always recognize the most desired qualities in ourselves. For example, if you asked the truly kind people, "Are you kind?" I'm sure they would shake their heads. They might say, "I wish I were kind," or "I try to be kind," but they would point to their shortcomings or focus on moments when they behaved harshly. "See, I'm not a kind person."

Suppose we take the first principle and move it to the realm of prayer. The principle then becomes: Whatever we focus on in prayer, we become. If we focus on the qualities that delight God and that make us more dedicated and caring Christians, we become such people.

The second principle is that we can't tell when we've attained the qualities we seek. Others may perceive such traits in us and they may tell us so. But even if they tell us, we may not be able to accept their words or be ready to believe them.

In "The Great Stone Face," those to whom Ernest spoke recognized that he had become what he had most desired to see; Ernest himself, however, failed to see what he had become. Hawthorne ends the story by saying that after the old man finished his sermon, he walked slowly homeward, still hoping that some wiser and better man than he would appear, a man who would bear a resemblance to the Great Stone Face.

That may sound like a tragic ending. If we apply it to prayer, however, I think it's an uplifting message. It says that people like Ernest will continue to yearn and plead to see those qualities already manifested in themselves. They don't grasp that they have those traits—and that may be the work of the Holy Spirit blinding them. If they saw who they had become, isn't it possible that pride might sneak in and spoil the very things they most desire?

Here's a biblical example. God called Moses to go up into the mountain to write the Ten Commandments for the second time. He stayed in God's presence for forty days and nights and ate or drank nothing during that time.

"When Moses came down the mountain carrying the stone tablets inscribed with the terms of the covenant, he wasn't aware that his face glowed because he had spoken to the LORD face to face. And when Aaron and the people of Israel saw the radiance of Moses' face, they were afraid to come near him" (Exodus 34:29, 30, NLT).

Moses had no idea that he had changed, but the people knew. Moses' attitude makes it clear to me that if we seek to embrace the qualities that make us more godly, we don't keep checking for results and doing personality profiles on ourselves. We gaze at our goals and leave the results in the hands of divine grace. Our role is to pursue the best—to yearn for the qualities we seek most in our spiritual growth. The true journey involves the search—the longing—and not the results.

⇝

In other books, when I have written chapters about various people in the Bible, I have arranged them in the obvious way: chronologically, beginning in the Old Testament. This time

I have chosen not to do that. In this book, I have written in order of discovery.

Here's what I mean. I start out by stating my hunger for God and then tell the method I've been using for the last three years. I don't look for people to identify with. Those desirable qualities grab me as I read my Bible. I "discover" in the sense that some outstanding characteristic strikes me, as if to say, "This is what I need." Therefore, in these pages, I'm presenting the stories in the order in which they came alive to me.

1

THE UNDESERVING

Three years after my conversion, I grew dissatisfied with my spiritual growth—or what I considered my lack of it. The yearning became increasingly strong and persistent, and no matter how much I prayed or read my Bible, the hunger didn't diminish. I finally went to talk to Pastor Arthur Dodzweit. In those days I didn't know how to effectively express what I was feeling, but I recall telling him, "I want to grow and to live on a higher spiritual plane."

He listened for several minutes and then urged me to read the Gospels and pay special heed to the words of Jesus. "Seek to be more like Jesus," he said, "and follow his example."

"Please don't tell me to be like Jesus," I said. "That's impossible, because Jesus is perfect. He's my teacher and my Savior, but I can't identify with him in his flawlessness." I pointed out that Jesus faced temptations, but he never experienced the taint of sin. Every time the devil tempted him, he stopped the aggressive move by quoting from the Bible. Jesus is the one I cry to in my need, and I know he hears me. "I love Jesus and follow him, but I can't be like him," I said. "I need to identify with someone who has experienced failure and sin and still keeps on."

My pastor expressed shock. I assumed no one had ever responded that way before. Finally he asked, "With whom do you identify?"

I thought for several seconds before I answered, "I'd have to pick David. He was power hungry, politically motivated, immoral, and he did a terrible job of raising his own children. No matter how badly he sinned, however, he always turned back to God. In his writings, I'm deeply touched by the intensity of his desire for God. Yes, I could identify with David."

Pastor Dodzweit suggested I read the Psalms and study the life of David. That ended our session. My pastor cared about me, and he meant well, but I didn't find much encouragement through his suggestions.

Over the years since then, I have talked to others about my growth and where to find help. The most common advice has been "Read your Bible more." Those answers imply that if I do more, I will receive more.

Perhaps this is true, but I sensed there have to be better ways to be enriched and strengthened in my spiritual growth.

Just before the end of the twentieth century, I came to a significant crisis in my faith. My theology taught me that God loved me—me and everyone else. I didn't doubt the biblical teaching. Emotionally, however, I didn't *feel* loved. God "so loved the world" (John 3:16) and sent Jesus to die for sinners, and that included me. Even so, sometimes I felt as if I were picked up and saved as part of a package deal. God had gotten stuck with me because of a sweeping compassion for everyone.

One time I tried to express this struggle to a prominent Christian leader. In response, he hurled Bible verses at me and struck me with a number of pointed logical arguments to convince me that I was loved. I couldn't break through to him that I knew the arguments. On a cognitive level, I agreed and could say amen to every affirmation. My problem wasn't my theology or my intellectual grasp. My emotions simply didn't agree. No matter how some belittle our emotions, they are powerful forces in our lives; often we act more from deep-seated feelings than from our reasoning ability.

The Christian leader admonished me to have more faith, to read my Bible more, and to pray more—typical, well-intentioned answers of the kind we tend to get. It's always "Do more" of something. That was the prescription: If I did more religious activities, everything would be better. He couldn't grasp what I was trying to say, and his response discouraged me from talking to anyone else.

One day I figured out a method that worked for me. It began over the same issue of not feeling loved by God. In my devotional reading I came across Romans 9:13, where Paul quotes God as saying, "Jacob I loved" (NIV).

That verse struck me as odd, even though I'd read it many times. The impact of those words stayed with me, and I pondered them frequently over the next few days. What did Jacob ever do to deserve love? Of all the people in the Bible, he was one of the biggest scoundrels and least deserving, and yet God loved him. He did nothing to earn that love and should have received severe punishment for the dishonorable things he did. Instead, he received God's love.

I wanted to be like Jacob. That is, I wanted to feel loved even though I felt unworthy and undeserving.

Pondering the story of Jacob caused me to think about Jesus' parable of the prodigal son. The father loved the younger son even though he demanded his inheritance, left home, and wasted all his money. When the son returned, the father embraced him, called for a feast, and gave him the best of everything. The boy wasn't hugged and blessed because he deserved those things. The father simply loved him and couldn't hold back his excitement. That's why there was joy over his return.

I wanted to be embraced like the prodigal. Instead, I felt like the older brother who stayed home, did everything required of him, watched his brother waste a fortune, and felt angry when the rebel received the hugs and a big celebration.

For most of my Christian experience, I had done what Christian leaders advised me to do—I constantly tried to do more of the religious things. I wouldn't have admitted to anyone during those years, and only much later could I admit to myself, that my frenetic activities were unconscious attempts to gain God's love. Or maybe they were attempts to prove to God that I deserved the blessings I had received.

As I pondered the story of the prodigal and the life of Jacob, I faced one sad reality: I couldn't earn God's love. The best I could do was to accept that God loved me. I didn't know how to do that, but I kept thinking of the deeply loved but utterly undeserving Jacob. To my amazement, one morning I heard myself praying in deep anguish, "I am Jacob. I am Jacob."

The more I thought of those words and focused on what I was saying, I knew that was exactly how I needed to pray.

"I am Jacob, whom you love." Several times I spoke those words aloud.

I prayed exactly those words every day for months. As I prayed, I allowed myself to envision what those words meant.

I could picture a son being embraced by a father. In my mind, no matter how much the wastrel protested, the loving parent kept saying, "I love you and that's what counts."

One day I was nearly through with a six-mile run, and instead of saying, "I am Jacob, whom you love," I heard myself say, "I am Jacob. I really am."

I had focused on *being* Jacob for so long that I had *become* like Jacob. That is, I knew I was loved. The powerful assurance was there in a way I had never experienced before. In that sense, I was indeed Jacob.

As I finished my run, I thought of "The Great Stone Face," which I had read during my teen years. I realized that the story presented exactly the concept I had now grasped. I went to the library and checked out a collection of Hawthorne's stories to read it again. Ernest had focused on one thing, and eventually he embodied the qualities he yearned for.

I've also thought of two of Paul's admonitions to the Corinthians. In one place he writes, "Even though you have ten thousand guardians in Christ, you do not have many fathers, for in Christ Jesus I became your father through the gospel. Therefore *I urge you to imitate me*" (1 Corinthians 4:15, 16, NIV, author's italics).

He didn't imply that he was sinless or perfect. But he zealously followed Jesus Christ. If the Corinthians, in turn, followed Paul, he would point them more fully to Jesus.

In 1 Corinthians 11:1 the apostle writes almost the same thing: "Follow my example, as I follow the example of Christ" (NIV). If we were to say this, it would sound like boasting. But Paul wanted the Corinthian believers to know that if they followed his example and his lifestyle, they would see an embodiment of godliness that pointed toward the perfect god-liness of Jesus Christ.

What would it be like to imitate the example of Paul? Or the examples of other outstanding believers in the Bible? What if I saw qualities in them that I yearned for in my own life? How could I embody those same qualities?

I knew I was moving in the right direction. For a long time, however, I didn't tell anyone about what I called my "experiment." I thought others would laugh at what I was doing. Yet I knew that this method had worked for me, and I had changed.

After that, I began a series of further prayer exercises. For periods at a time—often just a few days, but usually lasting several weeks—I chose one individual in the Bible whom I admired. I created a mental image of that person as if I could see him or her standing in front of me.

I tried not to ignore any of the person's shortcomings, because those made the character more human. I focused on a single, major quality I respected about that individual. If I was going to be like biblical characters, I wanted the experience to be like that of Ernest, who unconsciously turned into the Great Stone Face.

Each day, as I prayed, I imagined myself taking on the quality I had selected.

This may speak of my weakness, but I just couldn't—then or now—focus on Jesus as the role model for the qualities I wanted. I needed flesh-and-blood, sinful-but-saved creatures who embodied the attributes I sought to develop.

I write this even though I still hear people quote "WWJD" (What would Jesus do?). That doesn't work for me. Their question comes from a novel written more than a hundred years ago called *In His Steps*. A dozen people covenanted to ask, "What would Jesus do?" before they made any decision.

Why didn't that work for me? "I have no idea what Jesus would do," I said when I had to defend my nonuse of WWJD. "Jesus is perfect and without sin. I'm blinded by my own selfish, hidden desires." Sometimes I added, "I have an amazing ability for self-deception. Too often my heart is so filled with my desires that I'm not open enough to hear the voice of the Savior."

I did discover, however, that I could relate to other flawed human beings. The Bible is filled with them—and many of them stand as our leaders or guides to spiritual maturity.

For example, I suspect Paul was a hot-tempered zealot whose words sometimes cut his enemies to shreds. I have some of that quality in me, so I understand his struggles. In spite of that, he also embodied a boldness for God that I yearn for.

Some may have trouble with my approach. They can't easily say, "I am Jacob." I could have said, "I want to be loved like an undeserving Jacob," which is what my words meant. But to explain to God (who needs no explanations) and to unravel all the words for greater clarity made my prayer cumbersome. The simple concept worked for me. "I am Jacob" sounded direct; it enabled me to focus.

Each day, as I prayed, I envisioned more clearly what it would be like to be fully embraced by God's loving arms. The more unworthy I felt, the more I could appreciate that love.

In my case, this went on for months before the realization struck me that I had become like Jacob. That is, I felt deeply loved and fully accepted, without any qualifications and despite my shortcomings. Those simple words changed my life and escorted me along the path of closer intimacy with God.

Here is how I pray every day now. As I become aware of a need to change, I search for the desired quality in a biblical character. Each day I continue to pray in my shorthand form. Or sometimes when I'm reading the Bible, I'm struck by the quality of a person and I think, *Yes, that's how I want to be.*

In each of the chapters that follow, I have selected one quality that I yearned for in one flawed biblical character. I erased the gender lines. "I am Miriam." "I am Hannah." Those prayers flow just as easily as "I am David" or "I am Samuel."

I invite you to experiment in prayer with me. As you focus on a quality you want to cultivate—love, kindness, boldness, or contemplation—focus on one of the giants of the Bible, and make it a matter of daily prayer to be like that person.

At the end of each chapter, I've included a few sentences to amplify the idea. For me, these express the yearning of my heart. They are a prayer to God. I'm like Ernest, staring at the Great Stone Face, but with a difference: I want to be what I see.

(If you are uncomfortable praying, "I am Jacob," then pray, "I am *like* Jacob.")

I am [like] Jacob, whom you love.
I don't deserve your love. I can't earn it.
Thank you, God, that I can accept it.

2

THE SPONSOR
OF CHAMPIONS

I have a new biblical hero, and his name is Barnabas. For years I considered him an admirable figure. Now he's emerged beyond that, and I want to explain why.

The book of Acts contains four stories about him. Together, they show a remarkably compassionate man who encouraged others and who seemed able to see beyond what others grasped. He's one of the few people in the Bible about whom we read nothing negative. Whether his flaws showed or not, merely being human makes him imperfect and yet worthy of imitating.

The first story takes place a short time after the birth of the church. Christians—still a small cluster of Jews who had become followers of Jesus—engage in a form of communalism and mutuality: "Now the whole group of those who believed were of one heart and soul, and no one claimed private ownership of any possessions, but everything they owned was held in common" (Acts 4:32, NRSV).

The writer Luke also notes: "There was not a needy person among them, for as many as owned lands or houses sold them and brought the proceeds of what was sold" (verse 34).

Luke concludes this section of his account by almost incidentally mentioning a Levite named Joseph who sells a field and brings the money to the believers. From the way Luke describes this event, it implies that Joseph is the first to take that bold step. At least, it's the only specific example he mentions.

We also learn that due to Joseph's act of giving generously, the believers in Jerusalem give him a new name: Barnabas. Whenever a name change occurs in the Bible, it's like a drum roll to signify something important is going on. Joseph was already a perfectly good name with a long history, belonging to the son of Jacob and to the husband of Mary. The name Joseph means "May Yahweh (or Jehovah) add or increase."

The custom of changing names holds special significance in the Bible. Part of it comes from the fact that ancients put a great deal of thought into names, and their choices had nothing to do with pleasant sounds or popular labels. They named their children to commemorate events, to honor an ancestor, or sometimes to call attention to a significant event at the birth itself. For instance, Esau ("red") acquired his name because of his color at birth, while Leah ("weak eyes") got hers probably because of a squint or something abnormal with her eyesight. Some of the chosen names were intended as prophetic or to embody dreams for the child.

Whenever any person in the Bible gets a change of name, it alerts readers to take notice. We can expect that a change in the person's character or latent abilities will emerge. It's as if God says, "This is someone to watch."

When the early Christians changed Joseph's name, they must have observed a powerful quality in him—a quality that becomes more evident as his life unfolds. Barnabas means "son of consolation" or "son of encouragement." But that's not quite enough of an explanation.

Bar—the first part of the name—literally means "son of," but that's not what they were really saying. The Hebraic expression "son of consolation" would translate in English as an adjective, so that they really called him "Consoler," or an encouraging person. That new name hints at his future work. In this first account, he gives generously, but I think the early Christians see his action as more than donating money and possessions to the needy. After all, they didn't change everyone's name. No, there had to be something more.

What was it? Could it be that they grasped the motive behind the offering? Did they realize that Barnabas was not just offering possessions but was unreservedly giving of himself?

The next chapter of Acts records a disastrous story—a kind of follow-up—about a husband and wife named Ananias and Sapphira who apparently try to imitate Barnabas. They sell land they own but give only part of the money they had received for it, which was their right. However, they try to offer part and claim it's the whole. They attempt to deceive Peter and the other apostles, but the Holy Spirit reveals their deception. They had tried to imitate the encourager, but they didn't have the heart or commitment of Barnabas.

After that account, Barnabas's name disappears from Acts for a few chapters. Perhaps Luke did it that way intentionally, but I wonder if it's not a tribute to Barnabas's character not to follow his activities. The evidence in the Bible points to him as a promoter of others—one who championed budding leaders long before anyone else recognized their values.

Part of what makes me focus on this concept is that I helped a modern-day Barnabas named Alan Ross write a book aimed at the business community called *Unconditional Excellence*.[1] A major point of the book is that true leaders "sponsor champions" (his words). They see the good, the strength, and the ability in others. Ross stresses that they recognize ability among their peers—perhaps the person at the next desk—and they help to promote or sponsor those individuals. They go out of their way to promote their recognition, push open doors, and point out their qualities to managers and bosses. Champions themselves, they prove it by telling others who can assist champions-in-process reach their goals and be fulfilled. Alan Ross often said he loved to sponsor champions. As I listened to him, it occurred to me that he has the same spirit as Barnabas of old.

My working with Alan pushed me to reflect on Barnabas.

The second appearance of this man occurs in Acts 9, and that is where the character of the Encourager truly emerges. When Paul (then called Saul), in his zeal to persecute followers of Jesus, heads toward Damascus, a light appears from heaven that blinds him, and he plunges to the ground. Three days later a believer lays hands on him and prays for him, and Paul's sight is restored. Even more, the persecutor becomes the believer. He then travels around Damascus, preaches about Jesus, and amazes everyone.

---

1. Alan Ross, Unconditional Excellence *(Avon, MA: Adams Media, 2002)*.

Eventually, Paul the persecutor becomes Paul the persecuted when angry Jews seek to kill him. He escapes from Damascus and travels to the center of the Jesus activity—Jerusalem.

Here's how Luke explains the situation: "When he [Paul] had come to Jerusalem, he attempted to join the disciples; and they were all afraid of him, for they did not believe that he was a disciple" (Acts 9:26, NRSV).

The story could have ended there, and a disillusioned Paul might have disappeared from the scene, but God raised up a champion sponsor. "Barnabas took him [Paul], brought him to the apostles, and described for them how on the road he had seen the Lord, who had spoken to him, and how in Damascus he had spoken boldly in the name of Jesus" (Acts 9:27, NRSV).

I have no idea how Barnabas heard the news—or perhaps all the disciples had received the same information. Regardless, only Barnabas sponsors him. That one voice cries out, "Believe him!" Because it was the Encourager who speaks, they listen. That small bit of information tells us how readily others recognize Barnabas, and we glimpse his powerful influence on the early church.

After sponsoring Paul, Barnabas disappears again from the chronicle of the church's growth until Acts 13. Luke says that the leaders met in Antioch and among them were "prophets and teachers" (13:1). Guess whose name appears first on that list. It's the Encourager. As the leaders pray and fast, Luke says, the Holy Spirit speaks to them: "'Set apart for me Barnabas and Saul for the work to which I have called them.' Then after fasting and praying they laid their hands on them and sent them off" (verses 2–3, NRSV).

The two men start out on what scholars refer to as Paul's first missionary journey. Note the order of names. Before the journey, it is Barnabas's name that appears first; later, it is Paul's. Once Luke starts to write about the travels, he reverses the order and aims the klieg lights on Paul, the rising star of Christendom. After that, Paul's name always appears first and the Encourager's second. Sometimes Barnabas isn't even named.

This is where the true champion shines. The man Barnabas sponsored soon overshadows him, and he is no longer the star. It becomes Paul's show, and Luke relegates Barnabas to the status of a supporting player. For anyone who reads chapters 14 and 15 of Acts, this man is always listed second. It's always ". . . and Barnabas."

How do you think Barnabas felt about that? If Barnabas read Luke's account, I think he smiled. This is how encouragers function. They don't need to be in the spotlight or to stand out as the top player. That's not their role; they're there to encourage and to sponsor champions. To do so means they must get behind others—and that often means to walk in the shadow of men like Paul.

≶

Barnabas's real test was yet to come. Along with him and Paul on the first missionary venture was a young man, John Mark, who was the nephew of Barnabas (Acts 12:25). Their evangelistic efforts form a pattern—they preach, miracles happen, persecution results, and then anger intensifies against the apostles. They flee the city. No matter what happens, the evangelistic team moves from one place to another.

Only one incident mars the powerful impact of this story: "Then Paul and his companions set sail from Paphos and came to Perga in Pamphylia. John [Mark], however, left them and returned to Jerusalem" (Acts 13:13, NRSV). (Notice that Luke lumps Barnabas along with Paul's other companions.)

About two years later, Paul and Barnabas return to the church leaders in Jerusalem and sit through a long council meeting. After lengthy discussions, the leaders decide that Gentiles (non-Jewish believers) don't have to obey the Mosaic Law. The two evangelists return to Antioch, and after a period of time, Paul asks Barnabas to go with him to revisit the churches they had started. (Notice, Paul is now in charge.)

Then trouble erupts: "Barnabas wanted to take with them John called Mark. But Paul decided not to take with them one who had deserted them in Pamphylia and had not accompanied them in the work. The disagreement became so sharp that they parted company; Barnabas took Mark with him and sailed away to Cyprus. But Paul chose Silas" (Acts 15:37–40, NRSV). This short description displays Barnabas at his best.

A couple of years earlier, he had sponsored John Mark as an emerging champion. That young man went along to learn and to minister, but he just didn't make it. He quit the ministry.

Discouraged? Fearful? Hard to get along with? The Bible never explains what went wrong in John Mark's case. We know this much: John Mark gave up, but Barnabas didn't give up on John Mark.

That's a powerful moment for the Encourager. He had picked a person to sponsor, and one failure or one setback doesn't discourage Barnabas. He is still there to wrap his arms about John Mark. (If I had been the younger man, I would have been so filled with shame over my failure that I would have needed a Barnabas to sponsor me or I wouldn't have tried it again.)

Barnabas and John Mark leave to revisit the believers. Luke records that Paul takes Silas and they travel into new territory. That's the last time Barnabas is ever mentioned in the New Testament.

There is, however, one incidental verse that would have made the Encourager smile. It occurs near the end of Paul's life. The venerable old apostle is going to die, and he is quite aware of it. He writes a second letter to Timothy, his son in the faith. This is also the last writing of Paul—his farewell words to Timothy and to the world.

He joyfully anticipates his death and writes, "As for me, I am already being poured out as a libation, and the time of my departure has come. I have fought the good fight, I have finished the race, I have kept the faith" (2 Timothy 4:6, 7, NRSV).

Then we read one of the most powerful sentences in this letter. After Paul writes his final instructions to Timothy, he adds, "Get Mark and bring him with you, for he is useful in my ministry" (verse 11).

Barnabas had it right. Paul's final statement vindicated the Encourager's judgment. Mark had redeemed himself, and Paul called him useful. What a shining tribute this is to the man who spotted the champion—the man whom Barnabas wouldn't allow the chance to fail.

Tradition says that the second Gospel, Mark, was dictated by Peter but written by a one-time failure.

Barnabas understood. He saw what others did not see, and he never failed the champion he sponsored.

⇝

If I could write a letter to the Son of Encouragement, here's what I would say:

Barnabas, you are my hero.

You understand others' weaknesses and failures, but you don't give up on them. You sponsored champions like Paul and John Mark—and I suspect there were a lot of others we don't know about. You had the ability to spot them before anyone else did. More than recognizing giftedness, however, you stayed around to defend and to sponsor them. You were the special friend they needed.

You're also my hero because you didn't need to have the praise and applause for being the champion sponsor. You simply did the right thing—you sponsored talented individuals. Maybe that's why you were such a great sponsor. You were a champion yourself, and your compassion was for others.

Barnabas, I want to imitate you because you're the best!

> *I am Barnabas.*
> *I see abilities in others and sponsor them.*
> *Enable me to walk away so they don't have to*
>   *share the spotlight with me.*
> *Help me also to stand with them when they fail.*
> *Thank you, God of grace, that you help me to*
>   *help others.*

3

TRANSFORMATION
OF THE FEARFUL

I'm sure that Timothy sounds like an odd choice to take as a model. If we read between the lines of Paul's two letters, we discover a man with many flaws.

For one, he was probably quite timid. Paul urged him not to be afraid, to stir himself up, and to know that fear wasn't something that emanated from God (2 Timothy 1:7). Paul also exhorted him to be strong (2 Timothy 2:1).

During Paul's second missionary journey, Timothy actively evangelized at Corinth. Later, when problems broke out among the Christians of that city, Paul sent Timothy and perhaps Erastus to resolve the difficulties (Acts 19:22). The mission failed. It may have been because of Timothy's timidity (1 Corinthians 16:10, 11). Paul then sent the more forceful Titus, who calmed the situation (2 Corinthians 7).

The young convert probably didn't assert himself much, or Paul wouldn't have had to push him to stir up his spiritual gifts. Besides the possible timidity, Timothy may have had a number of physical problems. We think so because Paul urged him to try a little wine because of his stomach troubles (1 Timothy 5:23).

Because his father was a Greek (his mother was Jewish), Timothy may have involved himself in a physical regimen at the gymnasiums. And he may have gone too heavily into that realm, because Paul pointed out that, although physical exercise was of some value, godliness was valuable in every possible way.

I've made quite a list that would make most people turn away from imitating Timothy. I can give only one reason to pursue the example of that disciple—and that's why I can pray, "I am Timothy."

Here's why I want to imitate Timothy: *he was teachable.*

He was a convert of Paul on the second missionary journey and traveled with the great apostle through some of the most harrowing times. Another young convert named Demas left, but Timothy stayed. Paul even referred to Timothy as his spiritual son—quite an accolade (1 Timothy 1:2).

Timothy battled physical problems, was timid, and was not an assertive leader, but Paul never gave up on him. Paul even wrote two letters to the young man that we have as part of the Bible.

I find a lot of encouragement from looking at the example of Timothy. Here's how I see him. He was young—Paul even has to exhort him not to let people talk down to him because they are older. How could such an obviously misfitted individual be so special to the apostle?

What got me appreciating and understanding Timothy was that I remembered a seminary student named Orlo.[2]

I'll never forget the first time I heard Orlo preach. He was boring and stumbled over his words, and at times I couldn't

---

2. *Not his real name. Whenever I use only a first name in an illustration, this indicates I have changed the name and minor facts.*

follow the logic of his argument. He graduated at the end of my first year of seminary. I remember him because each week two students preached their senior sermons, and we were required to attend. The preaching exercises went on for fifteen weeks. At the end, I still remembered Orlo's as being the worst of all the senior sermons. I even wondered why the seminary would let him graduate if he was so bad.

A few years later, I visited a church's weekly dinner. After the food, they announced that a visiting minister would speak to us. To my surprise, Orlo spoke that night. After the pastor introduced him, I prepared my mind to sit in quiet boredom, and I hoped he would give us a brief—very brief—message.

To my amazement, Orlo delivered an outstanding sermon. I sat mesmerized and wondered what had transformed him. How could anyone change so much in such a short time?

After the service, I chatted with Orlo for a few minutes. I didn't tell him how bad I thought he had been at seminary, but I kept telling him how impressed I was at his progress. I didn't know what had changed him. I knew only that he had changed. And it made me wonder if those who taught homiletics had seen something latent in Orlo that didn't come across in his senior sermon.

The only thing Orlo said to me was, "I know I wasn't a good preacher in seminary, but I've been working at it, and I'm a little better now."

"No, you're a lot better," I said.

The story of Orlo helps me think of Timothy. He had many of the flaws we don't like in church leaders. But Paul—and certainly God—saw something in him that may not have been apparent to everyone.

Timothy persisted. He kept on and never allowed his short-comings to sidetrack him. We don't know the end of his story; however, around A.D. 325, the church historian Eusebius wrote that Timothy had been the first bishop of Ephesus. If that is true, the always-teachable disciple had ended up as one of the great teachers of the early church.

Yes, he was teachable!

"I am Timothy."

His story gives me hope. I don't mean hope of becoming a great preacher or church leader. But I have prayed to be like Timothy and have focused on the attitude of the man who many might have wanted to push aside, discourage, or dispel. He kept on—and he did more than keep on. I like to think of him as someone like Orlo who nurtured and developed the gifts he had received from God.

As I continue to grow in my faith, I want to develop every talent that God has given me. I want to become everything I'm capable of being. I want to be a lifelong learner.

"I am Timothy."

I can learn; I'm determined to grow. Timothy had a mentoring Paul to encourage him, to admonish him when needed, and to be there to love him. I have a few such people in my life, beginning with my wife and my best friend, David. Like Paul, they nudge me, rebuke me when I need it, and wrap their arms around me when I feel hesitant or fearful.

"I am Timothy."

I am growing. I am changing. As I continue to develop my talents, I'm thankful for the Pauls in my life who saw those abilities long before I did. For example, years before I ever tried to write for publication, a missionary named Joan Wheatley told me I could write. So did my wife, Shirley. Ben Kline, one of my professors in seminary, once remarked off-handedly, "You write good papers." I listened to him, not really sure, and a large part of me remained fearful and doubtful, but one day I began to write.

Charlie Shedd, a man now in his eighties, saw my first attempt. He wrote me a letter—which I still have—and told me that I was as talented as anyone he had taught in a long time and that I should keep writing. I did.

"I am Timothy."

I won't become a bishop and I won't be a dynamic preacher like Orlo. But I can become the fullest me—the most mature and developed Cec Murphey I'm capable of being.

> *I am Timothy, who felt fearful and inadequate.*
> *Grace-giving God, through your encouragement*
>   *and that of others you have sent to me,*
>   *enable me continue to grow and fulfill the*
>   *potential you endowed me with.*
> *Keep me teachable.*

4

WALKING WITH GOD

To "walk with God." What does that phrase mean? The statement appears only once in the Bible and refers to just one man. It occurs in the first of two references to the man in the entire Bible: "Enoch walked with God; then he was no more, because God took him away" (Genesis 5:24, NIV).

Here is the other statement about Enoch, which occurs in Hebrews 11:5: "By faith Enoch was taken from this life, so that he did not experience death; he could not be found, because God had taken him away. For before he was taken, he was commended as one who pleased God" (NIV).

Every time I read that statement about Enoch walking with God, I'm intrigued. Many times I've wondered, *What would it feel like if God said, "Cec Murphey walked with God"?* This doesn't imply that other followers of God aren't faithful and committed. God calls Abraham a friend, and David was a man after God's own heart. What makes this man Enoch different?

Translators have struggled with the verse in Genesis. The CEV interprets rather than translates the statement this way: "Enoch truly loved God, and God took him away."

Yes, it's obviously true that Enoch loved God, but the statement implies more. Or perhaps it implies a *kind* of loving—a loving without reservation, a loving that's pure and selfless.

I don't know precisely, but I yearn for that kind of relationship. What would it be like to be a person who walks with God in the sense Enoch did?

Perhaps the best way I can explain is to give examples.

Years ago, when my wife and I stopped at a gas station, my wife went to the restroom. About the same time that she went inside, so did another woman. A few minutes later, when they were washing their hands, the woman said to Shirley, "You're a Christian, aren't you?"

My startled wife said yes.

"I could tell by looking at you. There's something about you—something about the calmness on your face that made me know you loved God."

When Shirley related that conversation to me, it was the first time I had ever consciously thought about the way our presence reflects who we are (or *whose* we are).

As we drove on, I connected that insight with the story of Moses after he had gone up the mountain and spent forty days with God. When he returned, his face shone so brightly that the people made him put a veil across his face. Perhaps the brightness of his face had such a glow that they became aware of their own lack.

The way the story is recorded, it seems that the glowing of Moses' face wasn't a one-time occurrence. The Bible says that while he spoke with the people, he kept his faced veiled. "But whenever he went into the Tent of Meeting [the Tabernacle] to speak with the LORD, he removed the veil until he came out again. Then he would give the people whatever instructions the LORD had given him, and the people would see his face aglow. Afterward he would put the veil on again until he returned to speak with the LORD" (Exodus 34:33–35, NLT).

I want that kind of glow—not to make people fear or back off, and certainly not to impress people. I yearn for a relationship with the God of the universe that is so deep and intense that people sense the holy presence in my life.

As I wrote those last words, I asked myself again, *What would it be like to walk with God as Enoch did?* I can't possibly know, of course, but I can give my version.

If I walked that intimately with God, I wouldn't need God to speak to me. Our relationship would be so close that I would sense the divine will. I'd know and not even be aware of how I knew. The closest I can come to explaining this is to look at my own marriage.

At times I can look at my wife and know she's in pain or is tired. Once in a while, I have walked into the house, looked at her, and said, "Let's go out to eat."

"How did you know I was just going to suggest that?" she asked.

My answer: I didn't know. It just felt right to make that suggestion. In such instances, some intuitive part of me worked, and Shirley and I were in some powerful but nonverbal contact.

I yearn to be in such powerful contact with God that I'll know the divine will without any words or direction. I would know without knowing how I know—or caring how I know.

Most Christians have had a few experiences of this kind of intuitive knowing. Here's one example. Years ago, a group of us helped our friend Suzanne Stewart write her first book. The week after she finished it, she came to us and announced, "I've already sent it to Zondervan, and they'll publish it."

Most of us hurriedly tried to explain how the process worked and that they might reject it. One of us pointed out that, as one of the largest publishers, Zondervan received thousands of book manuscripts every year.

"They'll publish my book. I know it." She didn't say, "God told me."

No matter how much we tried to soften the blow for Suzanne, she remained adamant. She couldn't explain how she knew, but she smiled with an assured certainty. The best she could explain was that she had been praying for a few days and one morning she "knew" she should send it to Zondervan.

Less than a month later, she received a contract for her book.

That's a hint of the kind of intimate knowing I yearn for— and I want it all the time. I want to know in an unknowable, unexplainable way. I want the relationship that senses beyond the senses. For me, it also implies a relationship so personal that I would feel as if my will and God's were locked together. I could never say, as Jesus did, "I and the Father are one" (John 10:30, NIV). Yet as I ponder the possibilities, wouldn't that be close?

It would be the kind of connection that is realized in such a hymn as Frances R. Havergal's "Take My Life, and Let It Be Consecrated." The end of the first verse conveys the message:

Take my life and let it be consecrated, Lord
    to Thee:

Take my hands and let them move at the impulse of
   Thy love,
At the impulse of Thy love.[3]

Havergal's words have that kind of quality. It's a yearning that says, "I want more out of my relationship than I have now."

⇛

I've been praying to be like Enoch. I have no idea where this will take me. I also have no idea of my own spiritual capacity. I add that statement because I believe some people have a greater ability—call it a gift—for intimacy with God. For reasons we can't understand, they have an innate ability to snuggle with God. Or maybe it's just that divine arms hug them tightly.

If we're truly blessed, we meet one or two such godly people in our lives. We sense there's a holy presence about them. They're human and flawed and make mistakes like the rest of us, but they also have an indefinable quality about them. We can say of them that we know they've been with Jesus.

My yearning isn't so much that others will see my relationship with God (although I hope they will). My yearning is for an intimacy that is beyond any I've experienced so far.

In the old-favorite hymn "In the Garden," the writer says,

And the joy we share as we tarry there, none other has
   ever known.[4]

---

3. *The hymn was written in 1874.*
4. *The hymn was written by C. Austin Miles in 1912.*

That last phrase tantalizes me: "none other has ever known." The writer may have meant that the experience surpassed that of anyone else. I suspect, however, he meant the experience was so meaningful and life changing that words couldn't express how he felt.

Although I'm not sure what the poet meant, for me those words speak of a oneness with God that exceeds anything I could put into words. That's my picture of Enoch. That expresses my desire to be like Enoch and to walk with God.

> *I am Enoch.*
> *Like the one who walked with you, help me*
> *always seek to be with you on the deepest*
> *level of intimacy that I'm capable of as you*
> *increase my yearning for more.*

5

THE LIFTER-UP
OF TIRED ARMS

S trange that I remember this after all these years, but I do. I was twenty-five years old and had become aware of the dirty floor in the sanctuary of Christian Fellowship Church, where Shirley and I were members. It was a room about one hundred feet by fifty feet that had been built as a temporary worship center—twenty years earlier. The church had never grown, and all the furniture remained movable. I can still remember the gold and brown tiles and the grittiness under my shoes when I walked across an aisle.

I finally decided that no one else was going to strip the floor and rewax it, so I might as well. A college student at the time, I waited until I had a day without classes. The pastor gave me a key and brought everything I needed to clean the floor. I moved all the furniture out and went to work. Not only did I strip the floors, but in addition I laid down two coats of clear wax. The floor gleamed. Once I made sure the wax was dry, I carefully moved all the furniture back into place.

So far as I'm aware, not one person noticed the shining floors. The pastor didn't thank me or even acknowledge that

I had done anything. I admit (now) that part of my motivation for doing it was that I wanted to be appreciated for my labors.

Over the years I've been involved in other projects where I've labored and received no credit or little recognition. For example, one time in graduate school, the professor arbitrarily divided us into groups of five and gave us a paper to write. One member of my group did nothing; two of them did little. The fourth one did her research—that is, she did some research but couldn't seem to distinguish the important from the trivial.

The professor had appointed me as leader of the group. Finally I realized that if the group was going to receive a good grade (which was the grade each of us would receive for the semester), it was up to me. I took the minor contributions of the others, went to work, and produced a good research paper.

On the final day of class, the professor commended our group for writing an outstanding paper and asked us to stand up, which we did. The others commented on how hard they had worked and how they were delighted to have been part of the group. I was the last one—and I was in total shock that the others would take credit for work they hadn't done. I made an innocuous comment and thanked the professor. As we sat down, I wondered how those other four could stand up and take credit for my work.

Over the years I've learned there are always plenty of people who claim awards or jump up to receive undeserved acclaim. I've heard of men who were around during the Vietnam era and who never served in the military but who can tell powerful tales about battles they claim to have fought.

Beyond deceit, however, is the truth that we all want to be noticed, appreciated, and valued for our contributions. Maybe a lot of people have little or nothing to offer, and so they tread on the glory and achievements of those who do.

That makes it so refreshing to read about a man in the Bible who seemed not to have any need to push himself forward or have accolades addressed to him.

His name is Hur.

Unless you know your Bible well, you probably have no idea who Hur was. His name appears only three times in Exodus. (There were other men in the Bible by the same name, and they are just as obscure.)

Tradition says that he was the husband of Miriam, the sister of Moses. That may be true. The only times his name appears, he is with Aaron, who would have been his brother-in-law.

His major contribution is told in a simple story recorded in Exodus 17. Here's the setting. The Israelites have left Egypt and headed into Canaan, the land God promised. Problems have already surfaced within the nation—grumbling about food or not having water. Exodus 17 tells us the story of the nation's first battle.

"The Amalekites came and attacked the Israelites at Rephidim" (Exodus 17:8, NIV). Moses is the leader of the people, and he calls Joshua to gather men to go out and fight. Then he says, "Tomorrow I will stand on top of the hill with the staff of God in my hands" (verse 9).

The account goes on to say, "So Joshua fought the Amalekites as Moses had ordered, and Moses, Aaron and Hur went to the top of the hill. As long as Moses held up his hands, the Israelites were winning, but whenever he lowered his hands, the Amalekites were winning" (verses 10, 11).

Moses stands on a large bluff that overlooks the battlefield and holds up both arms with his staff in his right hand. As long as he keeps his hands high, the Israelites move toward victory. When his tired arms droop, the enemy prevails.

No one could stand with spread-out arms for hours, but that's what Moses must do if they are to defeat their enemy. They solve the problem when Aaron and Hur provide a boulder for Moses to sit on. The two men then stand on either side of him. Each man holds up one of their leader's arms. This goes on for hours until the Israelites defeat the Amalekites.

The Bible mentions Hur only once more, and that's in Exodus 24:14. Moses and Joshua go up the mountain and leave Aaron and Hur in charge. That statement implies that Hur must have been a man of ability to have authority alongside Aaron, who became the nation's first high priest.

Why don't we hear of Hur again? Especially if he was Miriam's husband and part of the elite leadership, shouldn't we have read more about him?

For me, that's what I admire about Hur. This is conjecture, of course, but the absence of further mentions of Hur implies that he did nothing to elevate or promote himself. He made himself available and held up his leader's heavy arms. Just that seemingly small thing, but without his being there performing that simple duty, the Israelites would have lost their first battle.

I like this aspect about Hur. He does the right thing, and there's no big publicity about it.

It's like doing the right thing and not caring who gets credit. For instance, I know a man who walks through the park near his home. He picks up empty bottles, paper trash, and cans. He said, "Nobody sees what I've done. They would only see it if someone didn't do it." He quoted the bumper sticker I used to see often: "Do random acts of kindness and senseless acts of love."

As I've pondered Hur's example, I've thought of other living examples of people who have held up heavy arms—doing little things that seemed small or insignificant at the time.

When I was a pastor of a church in a transitional community, I felt abandoned and rejected by most of the congregation. They had nothing positive to offer for correction, but they regularly offered negative comments on how bad things had become. One day an elderly widow named Louise Johnson told me, "I pray for you every day. I can't do much else, but I can do that."

That was a lot. I knew that at least one person (outside my family) cared. That knowledge strengthened me.

My friend Christine tells about the time she went to her first writers' conference. Within hours she realized how little she knew, felt discouraged, and wondered if she ought to go home. A stranger, Elaine Wright Colvin, walked over to her and said, "You look discouraged."

She talked to Christine, lifted up her tired arms, and guided her to courses and activities. Fifteen years later, Christine Tangvald's children's books have sold more than 2 million copies. But first someone held up her sagging arms.

I see a tremendous ministry in behaving like Hur. If we can move beyond our need for recognition and reward, we can lift many tired arms. We can help make the difference in whether others succeed or fail. We can add our strength to their waning energy and lift them high. To those who are too weary to go on, we can wrap our arms around them and say, "Let's go together."

> *I am Hur.*
> *Enable me to see needy, hurting people.*
> *Fill me with a yearning to lift those weary arms*
> *and encourage those sagging spirits.*

6

TOTALLY COMMITTED

I followed the Lord my God completely," Caleb said to Joshua (Joshua 14:8, NLT). That's a bold statement. As I read it again recently and tried to apply it to myself, I felt reluctant. Who am I to make such a statement? How do I dare to say that I have totally followed God?

Immediately, I thought of my failures—times when I lost my temper, when I argued or struggled to forgive, when I withheld compassion. In fact, I must have recalled at least ten failures in my life.

Then I realized something I had not thought of before: Caleb didn't claim to be perfect. He claimed only that he had followed God with all his heart and soul.

In that moment, I saw the difference. He wasn't trying to say to Joshua, "I've never had an impure thought," or "I've never spoken harshly to anyone." What he was saying was that he had committed himself to following God's leadership. In that he had not failed.

For me to apply the words of Caleb to myself was one of the hardest things I've ever had to do in my yearning for more of

God in my life. For several minutes, all kinds of warnings and alarms screamed inside my head. Did I think I was more committed than other believers? Who was I to boast of my spirituality? What made me think I was so good, noble, and faithful?

That's part of what I call my "religious baggage." During my years in the church, I've learned about sin and its pervasiveness. The problem is that somewhere I received a double infection of guilt that tainted my outlook. For years, I had the amazing capacity to feel guilty over almost everything I said or did.

My head yelled words such as "Pride!" "Super-pious religiosity!" "Hypocrite!"

Pushing those words aside, I spent a few minutes examining my life. I couldn't think of a single instance in my life when I had said no to God. I could think of once or twice when I sensed the Spirit speaking and it wasn't something I wanted to do. Even in those few instances, I said, "Nevertheless, at your word, I'll do it."

When I looked objectively at my life and filtered out the accusing tones, I thought, *Yes, I have obeyed and have wholly followed the Lord.*

Yet the teachings on sin came out at me from the corners of my mind. The most difficult part was to separate my sinful nature and my inclination to put myself first over the express (or implied) commands of God. Several more minutes passed before I finally had the courage to say aloud, "I am Caleb. I have wholly followed the Lord."

The first time I said those words I cringed inside, almost as if I had stood up in church and yelled those words and saw frowns and heard disgusted voices respond. I could envision pointing fingers and harsh rebuttals.

"I am Caleb. I have wholly followed the Lord." I said the words again and then repeated them several more times. By then, they felt a little more comfortable.

Throughout the rest of the day, I kept examining my heart and silently asking, "God, if I haven't wholly followed you, show me how to start."

This may sound strange, but as soon as I asked, I'd remember a specific act that I had done or something that didn't please God. The accusing words struck again, trying to keep me from rejoicing in my kinship to Caleb.

My emotions hit almost every level between completely positive and totally negative.

In the midst of that inner turmoil, I remembered something else about self-talk. Years ago a friend said to me, "If the words you repeat are not true, and you persist in saying them, you are telling yourself to make them true. You will begin to live that pattern." He also added, "And if you think of them as a prayer, God helps you make them true."

Was it a case of Ernest gazing at the Great Stone Face? Was this a goal I yearned for, and had already attained, but didn't know it?

Even as my fingers type these words, they are still troublesome for me. While I try to focus on a *principle*, my mind continues to run into *particulars*.

To help myself, I went back to the stories of Caleb. He isn't mentioned often, but each time, the Bible speaks about his heart—his commitment, his obedience, and his faith.

"That's it," I finally said. Caleb believed and obeyed. His obedience was such that he could say, without sounding boastful, "I have wholly followed the Lord."

Two things occurred to me. First, God said that Caleb had followed fully and faithfully. When Moses prepared the people to leave Mount Horeb and move into the new land, and he reminded them of God's disappointment and anger toward the people because of their repeated disobedience, he added, "Not a man of this evil generation shall see the good land I swore to give your forefathers, except Caleb son of Jephunneh . . . because he followed the LORD wholeheartedly" (Deuteronomy 1:35, 36, NIV).

Caleb hadn't boasted; he merely spoke the truth—words that God had already said through Moses. In fact, Caleb's words to Joshua many years later were only repeating what both of them had heard God say through Moses.

Second, no one contradicted Caleb. He was with family members when he spoke (although they might have been prejudiced), but he repeated the words to Joshua, who was then the great leader of Israel. He and Joshua had gone into the Promised Land as spies, along with ten other men. When they returned, only Joshua and Caleb said, "Yes, we can destroy our enemies. God is with us."

If that man had done less than he said—if he had turned away from God or failed to obey—who would have known better than Joshua?

At last I felt I had understood. When I say, "I am Caleb," I speak of my heart and my deepest desire. I refer to my hunger and my yearning for more of God; I don't refer to my human weakness.

Yes, I am Caleb. I have not turned back. I have wholly followed the Lord.

I yearn to follow God every day for the rest of my life.

> *I am Caleb.*
> *May I follow you completely.*
> *Increase my understanding of your way, that*
>   *I may follow you even more fully.*

7

SPEAKING FOR GOD

O nce in a while I think about heaven and being in the presence of God. A fantasy inside my head says I'm marvelously transported to that celestial place, and in my first conscious moment I stand before a glorious, overpowering light. I hear God speak the perfect welcome to me.

The greeting is a quotation from the words of Jesus when he told the story of three servants who were given different amounts of money by a wealthy property owner who then left on a long journey. After the owner returned, he asked the three men to give account of the way they had handled the money. The third one had done nothing but hide his in the ground, and he is rebuked. But for the other two, the owner says, "Well done, good and faithful servant! You have been faithful with a few things; I will put you in charge of many things" (Matthew 25:21, 23, NIV).

Good! Faithful! Those are the words I want God to speak to me. I want to feel that I've faithfully obeyed God in every way. I suppose every committed believer hopes to hear those words—and I'm sure many will. However, I'm confident one man mentioned in the Bible will surely hear those words. Everything written about him in the Bible, especially regarding his early life, sounds almost like a guarantee of it. His name is Samuel.

My admiration for that godly man began when I was twenty-three years old and had been a Christian only a matter of months. That's when I read the book of 1 Samuel for the first time. One statement stood out to me then, and I remember pondering those words off and on for years. Even now, no matter how many times I've read that book, the same message whispers to me. First, however, I need to set up the story.

Eli was the high priest of Israel, and the tabernacle, or temporary temple, was in Shiloh. Young Samuel came to live in the temple with the now-aged priest.

One night Samuel awakened when he heard his name called. Assuming it was Eli calling, he ran and asked what Eli wanted. The high priest hadn't called him. This happened three times, and the third time, Eli told the boy to say, "Speak, LORD, for your servant is listening" (1 Samuel 3:9, NIV). That's exactly what Samuel did.

When God awakened him again and the boy answered, God promised to shock Israel by punishing the family of Eli. He adds, "I warned Eli that sacrifices or offerings could never make things right! His family has done too many disgusting things" (1 Samuel 3:14, CEV). The next morning Samuel told Eli what he had heard.

The story then shifts to Samuel's life. To get the impact, I'm quoting the verse in context. First Samuel 3:19–21 reads, "The LORD was with Samuel as he grew up, and he let none of his words fall to the ground. And all Israel from Dan to Beersheba recognized that Samuel was attested as a prophet of the LORD. The LORD continued to appear at Shiloh, and there he revealed himself to Samuel through his word" (NIV).

The phrase "from Dan to Beersheba" is a way of referring to the entire nation, with Beersheba as the northernmost city and Dan located at the southern tip. It's as if Americans would say, "The word spread from Los Angeles to New York"—across the entire country. This passage wants to make it clear that all Israel recognized Samuel as God's prophet.

The problem with the verses quoted above lays in the use of the words "he" and "his." It's unclear whether the pronouns refer to Samuel or to God: "and *he* let none of *his* words fall to the ground."

The TEV translates this as ". . . and made everything Samuel said come true." That implies Samuel walked in such intimate fellowship with God that when he spoke he became God's mouthpiece and his words came directly from God.

This may be the correct interpretation, but I doubt it. Instead, I assume the verse means that "he" (Samuel) is the man of the promise who lives in such intimacy with Yahweh that he eagerly obeys everything God asks.

I opt for this view because a similar statement appears other places in the Bible, such as in the call of Moses, Gideon, and Jeremiah. The verb used in the phrase "fall to the ground" is similar to a statement about Joshua near the end of his life, even though it's usually translated as "failed": "Not one of the LORD's good promises to the house of Israel failed; every one was fulfilled" (Joshua 21:45, NIV). In 1 Kings 8:56, King Solomon declares, "Not one word has failed of all the good promises he [the LORD] gave through his servant Moses" (NIV).

In one sense it doesn't matter which interpretation is correct. Either way, we read a powerful statement about Samuel and his intimate relationship with God. He remained in such a committed relationship that everything he said happened just as he spoke. Or else it means God fulfilled every promise made to Samuel. Both interpretations make us aware of the spirituality of the man.

Another thing to notice is the way the author of 1 Samuel sets up the story by saying that the boy Samuel lived in the temple and ministered to Eli, adding, "In those days the word of the LORD was rare; there were not many visions" (1 Samuel 3:1, NIV).

That simple statement prepares us to realize that when God began to speak through Samuel, that wasn't an ordinary person or a commonplace event. It's as if the author whispers, "Pay attention. God didn't speak very much in those days. Something is going to change."

That change is the appearance of Samuel on the scene, and he becomes a model of faithfulness and commitment.

I find Samuel a personal role model because of the powerful statements the Bible makes about him there and elsewhere. Many times I've thought what it would be like to say that I've been so faithfully committed that God has made many promises to me and has fulfilled every one of them.

As I pointed out in the previous chapter, when I examine my life since I became a believer, I have no problem acknowledging my obedience. I can honestly not think of a single thing that God has told me to do that I haven't done.

That's not quite everything, however. My problem isn't when the Holy Spirit prompts me to do a specific act. In those instances, I'm open and I'm eager. My problem revolves around what I call the lifestyle will of God.

These are the commands that involve loving and serving others, putting away gossip or not speaking thoughtless, unkind words, and giving freely to someone in need instead of making excuses. ("He'll just waste the money.")

My struggle has to do with the day-to-day activities. Every once in a while I lose my temper, drive too fast, cut off another driver, or criticize those who think differently than I do. Do I know better than to act this way? Of course I do.

It's easy to excuse myself by saying, "That's part of being a human being and having the sinful nature within." I'll give a specific example of what I mean.

I know it's wrong to judge other people—judge in the sense of condemning or belittling others. When I was fairly new in the Christian faith, Shirley and I attended every service at our church. We belonged there and felt we needed to be there for ourselves as well as to encourage our pastor and other believers. That's the good part. The bad part is, one day I realized that I considered some of our fellow church members not to have really surrendered their lives if they weren't at church as often as we were. Although I didn't say so, I relegated them to Sunday-only believers, who were carnal or immature or didn't have the commitment that the rest of us did.

One day I was reading the parable Jesus told about the religious leader, the Pharisee, who boasted of all the good things he did for God. Then Jesus told about a tax collector who could only cry out, "God, have mercy on me, a sinner" (Luke 18:13, NIV).

I loved that story and the contriteness of the tax collector's heart. I liked to think of myself as crying out for God to have mercy on me. This time, however, I saw myself, not as the tax collector crying for mercy, but as the Pharisee, filled with pride over his accomplishments and commitment.

Is that a picture of me? Am I really judgmental like that Pharisee? Just asking the question was proof enough that I was indeed the Pharisee. I didn't want to acknowledge my judgmentalism. Like that religious leader, I could point to all the good things I did, from giving offerings to serving God. But I was like that man in the parable. Jesus said, "The Pharisee stood up and prayed about himself: 'God, I thank you that I am not like other men— robbers, evildoers, adulterers—or even like this tax collector. I fast twice a week and give a tenth of all I get'" (Luke 18:11, 12, NIV).

My sins weren't the same as those of the man in the story, but close enough. I felt ashamed and guilty. I was a Christian and committed to loving God and serving others. Was I really judgmental, or was I viewing the situation objectively? I tried to convince myself of the latter, but I wasn't very successful.

A few days later, as I prepared to teach my Sunday school class, I read the lesson, and it was Romans 14. Verse 4 made it feel as if an arrow had struck me: "Who are you to judge someone else's servant?" (NIV).

I cried out to God to forgive me for such an attitude. Yes, I had been the Pharisee. And I could say that since that day I've never been guilty of such an attitude again. But if I did, I'd be lying. That's where I have my weakness. It's not that I don't know the right things; it's that I "forget."

I could have told you a story about losing my temper or passing on unkind gossip. The point of all of this is my struggle with the lifestyle will of God. It's as if I have to keep saying, "Please forgive me and teach me again."

These are the areas where I need help and find myself calling for mercy and grace. I don't struggle with temptations to steal, commit adultery, or murder someone. My struggles involve the little things that I know displease God—the little things I tend to forget about.

Perhaps that's why the words about Samuel strike me so powerfully. God commanded and Samuel obeyed. There is never one word about what he didn't do or the failures he committed later. Every story in the Bible about that prophet-priest is of a man fully given to God. He didn't seem to wrestle with forgetting earlier lessons.

That's what I yearn for—to be so given to God that I can hear God's voice speak in the present. I also yearn to remember God's voice in the past.

I like to think of it this way: God chose Samuel and so used him that the whole nation recognized his uniqueness. That's a stirring testimony of one person's dedication and faithfulness. What would it be like to live in such harmony with the Lord that he constantly bestows blessing upon blessing? I can't think of a greater commendation than for God to say, "My servant, Cec Murphey, is so faithful that everything I ask of him he does faithfully. He lives the lifestyle that always remembers my will and never lets me down."

I am Samuel.
May I always remember your commands.
May my lifestyle exhibit you constantly at work
     in me.
I want to live in such harmony with you that
     I do the things that please you.

8

EMBRACING
THE VULNERABLE

The year after I graduated from seminary, I read a book by Father John Powell called *Why Am I Afraid to Tell You Who I Am?* With that slim volume, the author put into words one of my great concerns. He wrote, "If I tell you who I am, you may not like who I am, and that's all I have."[5] I understood that statement. That's what held me back—I didn't mind people knowing the real me, or opening myself to others, but what if they didn't like the person they saw inside? What more did I have to offer?

It's odd that those words struck me so deeply. Until then, I'd thought of myself as open. A coworker once said, "You're about as subtle as a pane of glass—I can see right through you." He meant that as a compliment.

What that book forced me to see about myself was the extent of my vulnerability. If anyone probed—about three inches—they'd find me transparent and candid. But if they tried to penetrate beyond my invisible wall, they hit a sheet of steel.

---

5. *John Powell,* Why Am I Afraid to Tell You Who I Am? *(Niles, IL: Argus Communications, 1970), p. 20.*

Powell's statement sounds negative, but it enabled me to face the reality of my attitude. I wanted to be open, but if I made myself transparent to others, then I was also open to rejection and misunderstanding, and people might not like me. And I wanted to be liked. I wanted approval and appreciation.

If people really knew who I was, would they still like me? That's the way I've heard the question asked by others. They ask that question because they're afraid the answer will be no.

In the days after I finished reading Powell's book, I thought of that question from the other side: "If I don't tell you who I am, you may not like who I am not, and you'll never know the real me." That was the dilemma. Did I want to subject myself to being misunderstood, disliked, or despised? If I were to become fully vulnerable, that's the risk I would take.

But isn't it worse, I asked myself, *to be loved for the wrong reasons?* Another comment I made to myself was this: *If they know who I am and don't like me, then it means they really don't like me anyway.*

Isn't it that simple? Of course it is, but it took me weeks of struggle to come to that conclusion. One of the things that helped me was that at the time I was doing a Bible study at our church on the disciples and early followers of Jesus.

One week I tackled Peter. How could anyone not like Peter? As we read accounts of him in the Gospels, he models the best and the worst in all of us. Several times he and the other disciples tried to push people away who clamored for Jesus. He's also the foolish one. Who else would see Jesus walking on the waves and cry out to come and join him—and then sink after a few steps (Matthew 14:22–33)?

Wasn't he the one who vowed, "I'll never betray you"? He said that the others might, but he wouldn't. Of course he did. Later, even after he became the great leader and chief apostle, Paul rebuked him for being hypocritical (Galatians 2:11–14).

He's the first of the disciples to grasp the truth about Jesus: "You are the Messiah, the Son of the Living God" (Matthew 16:16, TNIV). But he's also dense. In the next account Matthew presents, Jesus predicts his own death at the hands of the religious leaders.

> Peter took him aside and began to rebuke him. "Never, Lord!" he said. "This shall never happen to you!"
>
> Jesus turned and said to Peter, "Get behind me, Satan! You are a stumbling block to me; you do not have in mind the concerns of God, but merely human concerns." (Matthew 16:22, 23, TNIV)

I like it that Peter was among the three whom Jesus took with him everywhere—a kind of inner circle. For instance, he's at the Mount of Transfiguration. After the resurrection, it seems evident that Peter is the number-one apostle.

Yes, it's easy to like Peter. Maybe it's easy because he's so much like us at our worst and at our best. For example, if we read Acts 9, God had to speak to him in a dream and then interpret the dream before Peter finally caught on that God respects no individual. At his best and boldest, we see him stand against those who want him to stop preaching. At his most spiritual, he defies the deceitful lies of Ananias and Sapphira, and they die in his presence (Acts 5:1–11). Almost immediately after that incident we read, "People brought the sick into the streets and laid them on beds and mats so that at least Peter's shadow might fall on some of them as he passed. Crowds gathered also from the towns around Jerusalem, bringing their sick and those tormented by evil spirits, and all of them were healed" (Acts 5:15, 16, NIV).

Yes, it's difficult not to like Peter, and for many reasons. My primary reason for choosing Peter as one who pushes me to yearn for more of God is that he appears transparent throughout the Bible. He makes no attempt to hide his true self or to look better than he is.

In contrast to Peter, many people I meet work hard at being perfect. They don't want anyone to see their weaknesses or failings. They want us to like them for the image they try to project and not for who they really are.

I saw this quite clearly in writing for celebrities. For many years, I specialized in ghostwriting. That is, I wrote others' stories in first-person accounts. Some of them became wonderfully transparent and wanted to make it clear that they had made mistakes and weren't perfect. They were the exceptions.

Too many hesitated to let people see their dark side. One man in particular, a well-known preacher, refused to allow me to include information that would have made him more human, honest, and likeable.

"It will make me look bad," he said.

"It will make you look human," I said.

"Some people will misunderstand," he countered. "Some of them might stop supporting our ministry if they knew that." ("That" referred to something he did before his conversion.)

I lost the argument. He simply couldn't open up and let thousands of readers see that part of himself. In reality, he was unwilling to give anyone an opportunity to attack or censure him. He remained unwilling to let others know who he really was. I was convinced then and remain even more convinced today that people would respect him more if he had opened himself more fully.

I also understand his reluctance. It's not easy to be transparent, so I can sympathize with those who can't open up. Being vulnerable is something I struggle with. I used to say to my friends, "I want to be famous but not well known." I also realize, however, that when we show our true selves, most of the time people not only respect us but also identify with us. Even so, a voice inside my head argues, "But they might not understand." That's when I cringe.

For instance, when I was a pastor, I preached a sermon in which I said to the congregation, "I was wrong." I didn't try to justify my actions (it was an error in judgment more than a sin). At the door, a man shook my hand and said, "It's so refreshing to meet a pastor who is also a real human being like the rest of us."

Although I appreciated his words, I also overheard one longtime member say to another, "I don't come here to find out how weak a preacher is. I come here to be revitalized."

Guess which comment affected me the most? We tend to discount the positive and cringe over the negative.

I've learned a lot about God and about myself since those days. At this stage in my spiritual development, my attempts at transparency aren't for people to appreciate; they are part of my search for a greater intimacy with God. I live by the principle that the more open I am with God, the more it shows in my relationships with people. Or I could say it the other way: The more transparent I am with people, the more it helps me in being open to God.

Peter exemplifies that quality and makes me want to be like him. I realize from the stories about the apostle that his vulnerability gave him a wonderful, almost naive quality. Despite his failures, his rebukes, his weaknesses, and even his denial of knowing Jesus, Peter remained true to himself.

Perhaps that's one of the reasons he became the leader of the disciples. Is it possible that his vulnerability made him the man Jesus chose to be among his inner circle of three?

Although everything I've written so far emphasizes the powerful example Peter sets for me, there's one more fact about this man that touches me. After he denied three times that he knew Jesus, "the Lord turned and looked straight at Peter. Then Peter remembered the word the Lord had spoken to him: 'Before the rooster crows today, you will disown me three times.' And he went outside and wept bitterly" (Luke 22:61, 62, NIV).

He "wept bitterly." That's Peter. That's my hero. That's the man who makes me hunger for more of God. That's the disciple who is obvious and without guile—transparent. The word *transparent* means being capable of transmitting light so that objects or images can be seen as if there were no intervening material. I like to think of the transparent as those who hide nothing and remain totally, fully open. As we see into them and through them, we see the center of their lives—their love and commitment to Jesus Christ.

> *I am Peter.*
> *God, increase my transparency, so that the more*
> *open I am to myself, the more open*
> *I am to you and to others.*

9

THE TRUE BELIEVER

Help me to understand, God."

"Lord, I just don't get this. How can this be?"

"If God would only explain . . ."

Most of us have struggled with similar issues. No matter how we phrase them, we want to understand. We need to make sense out of chaos, problems, and events that don't go our way.

The events of September 11, 2001, stand out as one of those times when millions of Americans (and a lot of others as well) asked, "How can this be? Why did this happen?" Most of us invest a lot of effort into coming up with answers to satisfy us. One well-known preacher, for example, pointed to all the ways the people of the United States had turned against God's ways and then said, "What else could we expect?"

Did that answer satisfy people? I have no idea. I know that most of us are on a constant search, sometimes even demanding divine answers to things that don't fit with the way we believe they're supposed to be.

I wonder how many times I've listened to pastors who give up trying to explain and say humorously, "That's one of the first things I'm going to ask God when we meet in heaven." Not much of an answer, but it's a way of admitting, "I can't grasp this."

Most of us have a compulsive need to make sense out of life and events around us. We *have* to know. If we can't figure out reasons for seeming chaos, it may mean that life is truly chaotic and God is either effete or doesn't exist. Some struggle until they find an answer to satisfy their restless quest. Not that knowing will change anything, but there seems to be an insatiable drive to have the solution. "If you'd only let me understand," we pray.

I've prayed that way hundreds of times. A few months ago, I decided to stop asking for understanding. That decision moved me in the wrong direction. It was as if I said, "Help me understand, and then I'll believe." Or I could have said, "Then I'll obey." The idea of insisting on rational explanations may be our way of saying to God, "I don't trust you."

Our culture has elevated reason above everything else, and the need to understand demands vast amounts of energy. By contrast, one of the best examples of how to cope with lack of understanding comes from a young woman, maybe thirteen or fourteen years of age. She heard a message from God that she couldn't possibly grasp.

Her name is Mary. Most of us know the angel Gabriel appears to her and says, "You will become pregnant and have a baby boy, and you are to name him 'Jesus.' He shall be very great and will be called the Son of God. And the Lord God shall give him the throne of his ancestor David. And he shall reign over Israel forever; his Kingdom will never end!" (Luke 1:31–33, TLB).

She has only one question: "But how can I have a baby? I am a virgin" (verse 34).

The angel provides an answer, but it probably wouldn't have satisfied me: "The Holy Spirit shall come upon you, and the power of God will overshadow you; so the baby born to you will be holy—the Son of God" (verse 35).

I doubt that Mary understood the message even after she heard his words. But she asks no further questions, or at least none are recorded in the Bible.

I often wonder why Mary didn't demand a clear explanation—but then, that also points to my need to comprehend. To her credit, in some unexplainable way, the young woman accepts the promises of God without proof or clarification. God's messenger promises a supernatural conception will take place. Hearing the facts of what will occur seems enough for her.

Even though Mary didn't receive an unambiguous explanation, we understand the message because we've read the rest of Luke's Gospel and the story of the birth of Jesus. The child is born, and shortly afterward shepherds come to worship. They report to Mary and Joseph a message that angels gave them—they would find a baby in a manger. That would be the sign to them that the Savior had been born.

The shepherds spread the message everywhere. Luke writes, "The shepherds told everyone what had happened and what the angel had said to them about this child. All who heard the shepherds' story expressed astonishment" (2:17, 18). Their final mention reads, "The shepherds went back to their fields and flocks, praising God for the visit of the angels, and because they had seen the child, just as the angel had told them" (verse 20).

Luke records Mary's response to all the excitement and joy going on around her. He writes it so simply that it's easily missed. "Mary quietly treasured these things in her heart and often thought about them" (verse 19, NLT). The NKJV says it this way: "But Mary kept all these things and pondered them in her heart."

This is the picture of Mary that I find most powerful and that I yearn to imitate. She didn't understand—how could she? *She accepted what she couldn't grasp or make logical sense of.* She was content to ponder what had taken place.

This is an amazing story. A young, uneducated teenager hears the most preposterous message and says, "Okay, Gabriel, whatever you say." If I had been Mary, even after the shepherds' appearing, I would have insisted on credentials, proof, and a detailed action plan with follow-up details.

After Gabriel tells Mary that she, a virgin, will conceive and bear the Son of God, she responds, "I am the Lord's servant, and I am willing to accept whatever he wants. May everything you have said come true" (Luke 1:38, NLT).

Mary did one thing I admire: she believed. That's why I'm including her. I yearn to be like Mary. I long for the ability to believe without reservation and without any kind of proof. I want to be able to accept anything that comes to me from God and say truthfully, "Let it be so."

When I read about Mary's willingness to believe, it makes me want to be like her. I yearn for all doubts to vanish. I long to be able to trust God without first running the message through my brain to see if it computes with facts and common sense.

Sometimes I've justified my unbelief by saying, "If we can't doubt, we can't believe." That's probably true, of course, but it blurs the situation. I want to believe.

Maybe there's a reason we doubt—at least I finally figured out the biggest reason for *my* doubts. Deep inside is a nagging fear that God might not want the best for me. Part of it is a nagging fear that I'm not good enough or faithful enough to receive divine blessing and approval.

That's purely an emotional reaction; theologically, I know the truth. But in those times when I've been the most tested about believing God, doubts sneak into the dark corners of my mind and whisper, "What makes you think you're good enough?"

As I meditate on the response of that simple woman— totally unlikely to become the mother of the Savior of the world—I'm amazed at how easily she believed, especially without proof. That's the level of faith I want.

When I read the Bible, I want to believe everything without first understanding and making sense out of it all.

When I pray for guidance, I want the assurance that God does only the right, best, and holy thing for me. I want to trust like Mary. I want to be able to live a life where I constantly feel God's smile on my life because I believe. I want to accept whatever happens because I know the sovereign God is in control of the vast universe and also my tiny corner of the world.

I am Mary.
I want to believe without questioning.
May I be able to say confidently as she did,
    "I am the Lord's servant, and I am willing
    to accept whatever he wants."

10

DOUBTLESS FAITH

I wish God would wipe away every doubt. I yearn to trust God so completely that I never have to struggle or waver. God probably won't grant that to me, but I still pray for that to happen.

I wish I believed and never struggled with doubts. I wish I could accept everything about God, the Bible, and the working of the Holy Spirit in my life in such a way that I could rest totally assured without the slightest wavering of faith.

In the previous chapter, I pointed to one aspect—the need to understand before believing. Another reason I struggle is because I haven't fully overcome questions and doubts. As strange as it may sound, I doubt the generosity and grace of God. It's as if I think, *Who am I that God should see fit to bless me?*

Too often I'm like Gideon, wanting to make sure that God does want to use my life and my gifts. I want God to give me signs and assurances, to speak to me through dreams or other people—anything to make my spiritual pathway easier to follow.

I'm often more like King Jehoash, who visited Elisha at the end of the prophet's life. Elisha told him to take a bow and arrows and shoot them out the window. "This is the LORD's arrow, full of victory over Aram, for you will completely conquer the Arameans at Aphek. Now pick up the other arrows and strike them against the ground" (2 Kings 13:17, 18, NLT).

The king did what he was told—except that he struck the ground only three times.

"But the man of God [Elisha] was angry with him. 'You should have struck the ground five or six times!' he exclaimed. 'Then you would have beaten Aram until they were entirely destroyed. Now you will be victorious only three times'" (verse 19, NLT).

Call that little faith or call it doubt-riddled faith. Either way, the king failed the belief exam by striking the ground so few times. I probably fail most of my tests too.

As with Jehoash, it's not that I don't believe or that I want to fail, and I certainly don't want to doubt. But it's difficult to think of the lavishness of grace poured out on me. Theologically, I know we serve an extravagant, generous God who lavishes blessings on us.

For at least a year, almost every morning I heard myself saying, "God, why are you so good to me? What did I ever do to deserve this?" Yes, I know that grace means undeserved favor, but the question still lingers. If only I could figure out some method to be worthy, then the doubts would vanish—or so I tell myself.

When I was younger and spoke of wanting to trust God more implicitly, friends quoted Romans 10:17—and always in the King James Version: "Faith cometh by hearing, and hearing by the word of God." After quoting the verse, they exhorted me to read my Bible more faithfully.

It was always the do-more syndrome—if I did more, God would respond more favorably. I'm sure God honored my sincere desire and I grew. But unfaith always peeked around the corners.

I know that's not the way it works, and I have grown in my faith. Even so, doubts still linger. I've finally found some peace in this dilemma through an incident in the life of Jesus. A father brought his son to Jesus for healing. "Teacher, I brought you my son, who is possessed by a spirit that has robbed him of speech" (Mark 9:17, TNIV). He described the symptoms and commented that the disciples tried to heal the boy but failed.

Jesus cried out, "You unbelieving generation, how long shall I stay with you? How long shall I put up with you?" (verse 19). He obviously meant this as a rebuke to his disciples. Then he asked the father to bring the boy forward, and the father said, "But if you can do anything, take pity on us and help us" (verse 22).

Jesus then said what has become familiar to most Bible readers: "Everything is possible for one who believes" (verse 23).

"Immediately the boy's father exclaimed, 'I do believe; help me overcome my unbelief!" (verse 24).

Jesus healed the boy. Later, when the disciples asked why they couldn't perform the miracle, Jesus replied, "This kind can come out only by prayer'" (verse 29).[6]

Two things I've finally figured out from this story. First, the disciples had traveled with Jesus for months, were called to follow and do the same ministry he did, and watched the Lord perform miracles. Despite all they saw, and despite being in the presence of Jesus, they still couldn't perform miracles. It's too

---

6. *Some older translations add "and fasting," but those two words probably don't appear in the original texts.*

easy to say that this all happened before the coming of the Holy Spirit, as if that excused them. Jesus rebuked them, which says he had expected them to be able to perform healings as he did.

As sad as that account is, it encourages me to realize that I'm not alone in struggling with doubts. Even those who were the most exposed to Jesus' ministry also had problems.

A second thing I learned from that account was the honesty of the father. He didn't try to bluff his ability to believe. He had brought his son. Even if it was a desperate move on his part, he had come. He believed—and said so.

That father was honest enough to admit his lack of faith and cried out, "Help me overcome my unbelief!" That makes him a role model for me.

I want to believe. I want every doubt erased and pushed away. I don't know if that will ever happen.

By contrast, new converts used to amaze me (and I was once one of them). They took everything at face value. "If God said so, that settles it." They had no questions. They read the Bible and accepted every word. Perhaps that was a form of what I call magic faith. It's like children who believe everything they hear. If an authority says something is true, they have no doubts. They can easily accept Santa Claus and tooth fairies and parents never being mistaken. The time comes, however, when doubts creep in.

That's the way I see my own faith in God. I don't want to doubt; I want to believe. But at times unbelief creeps in.

I want to believe that everything that happens in my life is God's will, and then I can invoke 1 Thessalonians 5:18. ("Give thanks in all circumstances; for this is God's will for you in Christ Jesus," TNIV.)

I live somewhere between the extreme of constant doubting and the other extreme of unreservedly thanking God for all things and believing in God's unfailing provisions and love. That's the problem—I'm somewhere in the middle. I yearn to be able to say, "I believe, and my unbelief has vanished."

For the past few days, I've been visualizing myself as that father who wants healing for his young son. "I believe," he affirms. I yearn to be able to say, "I believe. You have taken away my unbelief." Surely when he watched the healing of his son, any unbelief had turned to seeing the truth of Jesus' power in front of him. His doubts vanished.

The more I focus on that father and compare myself to him, the more I realize I have the advantage of being able to read those accounts in the Bible; I've been theologically instructed. I've also had far more experiences with God's love and miraculous provision than had that poor father. He yearned for only one miracle; I yearn for a life of miracles and exciting experiences with God.

I take my cue from that father *after* the healing. Now he knows. He believes in the power of Jesus Christ.

Yes, I am beginning to see myself like the father. As I envision myself approaching God, I find strength in revising his prayer:

> *I am that concerned father.*
> *I believe—*
> *help me banish all unbelief and trust you*
>   *completely.*

11

THE INNER CIRCLE

One afternoon, as we talked about relationships, I realized that David had become my best friend. By then, we had known each other for at least fifteen years. Our relationship had begun when I was a pastor of a thriving church and David, a psychologist, taught at a local college. We met when he offered a two-day course for professionals on helping people after they had gone through divorce.

We connected during those two days and began to have lunch together. The more often we saw each other, the greater our mutual respect and affection grew. I don't think I realized how much I treasured his friendship until we moved from the Atlanta area ten years later. For the four years I was gone, we stayed in touch. During those years, we alternated Saturdays calling each other. Our relationship grew despite the distance.

Shortly after I returned to Atlanta and we began meeting regularly, I said, "You have become my best friend," and we talked about what that meant.

As he listened, David said one of the most insightful things anyone has ever said to me: "You were everyone's best friend, but you never had a best friend, did you?"

His words shocked me, and for several seconds, I mentally reviewed my friendships over the years. One by one I ticked off their names. I had called each of them my best friend, but deep within I had known it was a one-sided relationship. For too many of those years, I had been their best friend because they needed me. When they no longer needed me, I was no longer number one on their list.

"You know, you're right," I said, shocked to realize that fact.

Tom, for instance, used to call me regularly. For at least a year, we went to lunch regularly. We had gotten to know each other because I was a published writer and he wanted to be one. For a long time I remained oblivious to the fact that every time we met he asked for advice or wanted me to look at a manu-script. Once he began to publish, he stopped calling.

A situation developed and I needed someone to talk to, so I called Tom, the man I assumed was my best friend. When I asked if we could get together, he gave me some vague response about being busy but said he'd call soon. That was seventeen years ago, and I stopped waiting long ago.

I've learned there are always those who want to be our friends. They want us to include them in our select group of intimates and to be close to us.

I also believe some people simply don't have the capacity for friendship. Tom is one of them. I'm not sour or upset. The problem was my perception. I had invested him with something he didn't—and possibly couldn't—accept: my friendship.

This makes me realize that many of us don't have a true best friend—the one who truly loves us. Here's my definition of a best friend: someone who knows all my faults, still loves me, and has no plan for my self-improvement. David was the first person who ever met that standard.

I want to point out that I don't include my wife in this. Although many may disagree, I believe our spouses have different functions for us than our friends do. I see my wife as being "one" with me, as the Bible expresses it in Genesis 2:24. For me, at least, "best friend" refers to someone other than my spouse. It's having a relationship with a person who owes us nothing, who isn't married to us or bonded to us as a sibling or other relative. It's another human with whom we connect and our souls unite in deep loving affirmation, acceptance, and appreciation.

I see this modeled in the biblical story of Jonathan and David (1 Samuel 20). Another example I see is that of Jesus and John. Why else do we refer to John as "the beloved"? He never names himself in the Gospel that bears his name but writes only of "the disciple whom Jesus loved."

John was one of the three men in Jesus' inner circle. The Lord called twelve to follow him and spread the good news. Jesus chose the same number as the twelve tribes of Israel. They traveled everywhere with him. But three of them had special experiences with him—Peter, James, and John. For example, on the Mount of Transfiguration, only those three are with him (Mark 9:2–13). In the garden of Gethsemane, Jesus left the nine praying (and soon sleeping) and took the three with him. He was in such agony that he left the three and went and prayed by himself.

The revealing relationship shows when John describes the Last Supper. The NKJV translates John 13:23 this way: "Now there was leaning on Jesus' bosom one of His disciples, whom Jesus loved." Not only does it refer to John as loved, but the term "Jesus' bosom" means he was on the Lord's right—the special, reserved place.

That's my picture of John. That's the relationship I yearn to have with Jesus—to be the disciple whom Jesus loved. We are all loved by Jesus, of course, but that's not quite the picture I hold in my head. I'm thinking of the human Jesus who had friends, the man who loved Lazarus and wept when that friend died. This is the Jesus who loved everyone but had special relationships with a few.

All of us have a natural yearning to be special. We want to feel we're vitally important to at least a few individuals. We yearn for true intimacy with the Savior—a special relationship. I don't know if it's attainable, but that should not stop us from asking.

I want to be John—to be the disciple closer to the emotional side of Jesus than anyone else I know. I want to feel special, unique, privileged. I want to be designated as the disciple whom Jesus loves. Is it possible that all of us secretly wish we could be called by that term?

I don't know about that. But I do know that I can pray for the intimacy I yearn for. There are other ways to pray and express this desire for closeness, but I find it helpful to identify with John.

One more thing about John: the modesty factor. He doesn't tell us his name or in any way imply that he feels better, superior, or greater than the others. It's not an appeal to power or smugness in an elevated status. It's a statement of relationship. He truly feels special to his human friend, Jesus. That's what I yearn for—the relationship that, at least from my side, makes me feel especially loved and cared for by Jesus.

> *I am John.*
> *I am the disciple you love.*
> *I yearn for greater intimacy with you and a*
>   *closer commitment in every part of my life.*

12

TOUCHING THE NEEDY

Eighteen men met together for a two-day retreat in the mountains of north Georgia. Among our activities, I led studies to open the men up to themselves and to each other.

The first afternoon I asked them to read aloud the parable of the good Samaritan, found in Luke 10:25–37. Jesus used the story to explain to a lawyer and to others the concept of neighbor.

In the story, a Jew traveled from Jerusalem to Jericho. In those days, people simply didn't travel alone, because of robbers. Yet apparently the Jew was alone, and robbers not only took everything he had but beat him as well. As the man lies dying alongside the road, a priest sees him and then a Levite (also a priest but of a lower rank). Both men ignore the wounded man and hurry past.

Finally, along comes a man from Samaria. The listeners of Jesus' day grasped that point immediately because they despised the Samaritans. Back in the days when there had been two kingdoms, those from the north had their capital at Samaria, and the Assyrians overpowered them and took the leaders from the land.

Some Jews remained, and the Assyrians brought in Gentiles to mingle with them. Inevitably, they intermarried. From that time on, Jews hated the Samaritans because of their mixed blood and considered them worse than the hated Gentiles.

As the story goes, the half-breed spots the Jew, picks him up, and binds his wounds. He places the wounded man on his own animal and transports him to an inn. The next day he leaves the suffering man there and tells the innkeeper, "Take care of him; and when I come back, I will repay you whatever more you spend" (Luke 10:35, NRSV).

Jesus finishes his story by asking which man is the neighbor. The answer is obvious. However, that's not the question I asked the eighteen men in front of me.

"Think of the players in this story," I said. "We're told 'robbers' attacked him—meaning several—but for our purposes, I want you to focus on one of them. Here's the exercise. First, try to picture yourself as a robber and then as one of the men who passes by, then as the Samaritan, and finally as the innkeeper who takes care of the wounded man."

They nodded, and we spent a few minutes for them to reflect on the story. Then I asked, "Which of these people do you most identify with?"

Not surprisingly, all eighteen said, "The Samaritan."

For the next few minutes, we discussed what it felt like to be the Samaritan—the hero of the story, the one who is kind and loving and does good things for others. They leaped into the drama of the story, especially when I asked them to express their compassion for the wounded man.

We also discussed the two people who hurried by and then the innkeeper, but there was one more character I wanted them to focus on. "Why do you think none of you identified with the wounded man?"

I loved the expressions on their face as they struggled to tell me the obvious. "He was the victim." "He was beaten, defeated." "He was helpless." "He couldn't do anything to help himself."

"Have any of you ever been the man lying in the road?"

For several seconds (although it seemed longer), no one said anything. Finally two men responded. One of them had almost died in a construction accident five years earlier. "For eighteen months I couldn't even dress myself," he said. Right about that time, his wife left him. "I had to call on my friends and members of my church," he said. Tears glistened in his eyes. "I was thirty-seven years old, and I had to ask people to pick me up and take me to the toilet, bathe and shave me, and cook my food."

The second man told of the time his engine blew up on a lonely road more than two hundred miles from his home. While he was trying to figure out what to do, a family drove by, saw his problem, and helped him to get his car towed. By then darkness had set in, and they put him up for the night in their home.

"I was a stranger and they did that for me, and I kept trying to tell them how grateful I was." He said he offered to pay them, but they refused. "We're glad we were able to help," the father said.

As we talked, the men began to realize how difficult it was for them to depend on others. We in the Western culture pride ourselves on our self-reliance and don't like to depend on anyone.

Like the other men in the group, I felt extremely uncomfortable. I wanted to be the Samaritan—the helper. I didn't want to be the needy man.

As we continued to talk, eventually every man present admitted that, on some level, he did know what it was like to be helpless and in need. All of us struggled with accepting help, let alone asking for it.

That night I didn't sleep well. I kept thinking about the wounded man. Yes, I knew it was only a story Jesus told to make a point—and his point was really that the despised man was the true friend, the unexpected hero. That wasn't what troubled me that night. I kept thinking about the helpless man.

I hated the idea of being unable to take care of myself, of having to depend on others. I also realized I wasn't alone. The more I thought of that, the more I realized how much pride I have.

So far as I know, no one has ever labeled me as proud, because I'm not a boaster or the kind who constantly tells others how marvelous or gifted I am. No, my pride was more subtle. Perhaps a gospel song will explain it.

When I first became a believer, in the first church I joined, we sang a song with the words "It's Jesus and me." The idea is that, with Jesus by my side, I can handle anything that life hurls at me. I still believe that.

Pride crept in because I believed that Jesus was *all* I needed— I didn't need other people. As long as God was at my side, what else did I lack?

I wish I could report that as I lay there in the darkened room at the retreat center in north Georgia, I worked it out. The truth is, I didn't. Another three or four years passed before I understood the power of that story. I've told much of that event in a previous book called *The Relentless God,*[7] and I don't want to repeat it here.

The lesson I had to learn was not only that I am a needy person, but also that I should rejoice in my neediness. That may

7. *Cecil Murphey,* The Relentless God *(Minneapolis: Bethany House, 2003).*

sound strange, but I believe that's how God planned for the gospel to work: Each of us needs the others.

Paul referred to the church as a body (Romans 12 and 1 Corinthians 14). His point is that we have different functions, and all of us are there to support and care for one another.

≂

I want to approach this helplessness from another angle, drawn from a book I wrote. I often write other people's biographies, and they call me a ghostwriter because I try to write the book so that it sounds like the other person and it's done in first person.

One book I wrote is called *Ninety Minutes in Heaven*.[8] Don Piper, a Baptist pastor, was on his way home from a church-growth retreat in southern Texas. A truck ran into him and crushed his small car, and the emergency medical technicians pronounced him dead. Don went to heaven. Ninety minutes later, another pastor came along, and even though he knew Don was dead, he began to pray. Within minutes, the dead man returned to earth.

Don had so many physical injuries that they didn't know if he would survive. If it had been up to him, he would have gone back to heaven, but his friends began to pray for him to live. Over a period of years, Don underwent thirty-four surgeries. As he slowly came out of his ordeal, even when he was bedfast, caring members of his church wanted to do something for him. He always said no and thanked them.

One day a preacher friend said, "You need to get your act together." The friend railed at Don for his pride and his unwillingness to let the people help him. His friend said, "Let them

---

8. *Don Piper with Cecil Murphey,* Ninety Minutes in Heaven *(Grand Rapids, MI: Revell, 2004).*

buy you a milk shake or a magazine. Let them do something to express their love and compassion."

Even though Don knew his friend was right, he resisted for a couple of days. Don finally allowed people to reach out to help him, but he says that even today it is difficult for him to open himself up so that others can help.

When I began to work with Don, I went through that very thing. I needed help with a personal issue, and it took me a long time to ask others to do something for me. It's still not easy, but I am learning. God never intended for any of us to do everything for ourselves. We need others.

About the time I realized how I held back from others' helping me, I began to pray as if I were the wounded man. I realized how much help I needed from others. Of all the prayers I've prayed that I recount in this book, this was for many months the most difficult. I've always tried to be the person who was there to help others when they needed someone. But I couldn't admit that I was needy.

It took me months—perhaps a year—to pray the prayer below joyfully. Intellectually, I knew it was right the first time I prayed; emotionally, I didn't want to face my weakness, my helplessness. Now I can pray it—and in fact do so—regularly.

> *I am the needy man.*
> *I need help from you, God, but I also need help*
> *   from others.*
> *Thank you for making me open to my neediness.*
> *Thank you for sending people to minister to me*
> *   and my needs.*

13

FIVE-BAG PERSON

She's a well-known writer and one whose books I enjoy. One day I saw her on the TV program *Book Tour*. She spoke articulately about how hard she worked at her craft, and she knew she was good at it because she put the effort into it and rewrote her material at least five times. As she continued to talk, she implied that anyone could do what she had done.

As I listened and watched, I thought, *Yes, but unless you had a gift to write, could you have been that successful?* I didn't mean just to sell books, but I also refer to the quality of her writing. I had read her two previous books and admired her ability.

The interview made me ponder for quite a while. I may have misunderstood, but it sounded to me as if she were saying something like this: "I made up my mind to be a successful writer. I learned the craft and wrote books, and now those books have sold millions of copies."

Obviously, on a show like that, the woman couldn't say everything, but one omission bothered me. She mentioned her talent, her hard work, and her commitment. She never once spoke about where that talent came from.

I finally figured out that her lack of acknowledging her gift-edness is what bothered me. She's not unique. One thing that too many of us take for granted is our giftedness. Because we have abilities, it's easy to think of them as natural. Or that we have given them to ourselves by our hard work and dedication. Too often we fail to acknowledge that what we have has come from God.

This has become an important issue for me. As a reminder, every day, this is one of the things I say aloud: "Everything I am and everything I have come as gifts from God." Because I am a writer, writing is my focus, but the words apply as readily to masonry, accounting, or dressmaking.

Part of this writing about giftedness came about one day while I was reading another one of Jesus' parables. It's the one we often call the parable of the talents. It's unfortunate that the money was called a "talent." A footnote in my study Bible says it was a sum of money worth at least a thousand dollars today.

The story is quite simple and appears in Matthew 25:14–30. A landowner calls three trusted servants to him. He gives each a portion of money to invest. To one, he gives five thousand dollars (using the figure of a talent being worth a thousand dollars), three thousand to the next, and a thousand to the third. The landowner goes away.

When he returns, he asks for an accounting. The first servant had doubled his money and presented the owner with ten thousand dollars. The second had also doubled his. The third, however, was afraid of displeasing his master, so he buried the money in the ground. He hadn't lost anything, but he hadn't done anything productive with it either. The landowner called him lazy and wicked and says the least the servant could have done was put the money in the bank to draw interest.

To the first two, the master says, "Well done, my good and faithful servant. You have been faithful in handling this small amount, so now I will give you many more responsibilities. Let's celebrate together!" (verses 21, 23, NLT).

For me, the power of the story isn't the distinctions among the three servants but in what the master decides to do.

Here's how the Bible records this portion: "Take the money from this servant [the third man] and give it to the one with the ten bags of gold. To those who use well what they are given, even more will be given, and they will have an abundance. But from those who are unfaithful, even what little they have will be taken away" (verse 28).

Here's where the story hooked me. It's not enough merely to have abilities, but God gives them to us to use. To use means to sharpen them, make them more productive, and constantly find ways to make them useful for the Master.

In the story, the servants had gold, and their task was to make more money for their master. To us, it's not money, but it is about the gifts God has given to each of us.

I've observed many who have either hidden their gifts or used them sparingly. When I was a teacher in the public schools, I saw able teachers who did what was required—little more and often slightly less. "I put in my time" expressed the attitude, and I heard it voiced several times. I saw the same attitude when I was a temporary employee for civil service.

I could write about this in terms of pastors and writers, because they're the two fields I've been the most involved in. I learned early in my pastoral career (I was a pastor for fourteen years) how many ministers never tried to improve their preaching skill, didn't learn the new methods of teaching, and rarely attended continuing education courses. I'm not trying to belittle them, only to point out how this works practically.

For the past twenty years, I've been a full-time writer. I also teach writing in about ten conferences a year. It saddens me to see some of the same instructors teach the same lessons they've been presenting for a decade. They don't improve their craft, and I doubt they help others much. I'm sure what I say is true with any occupation.

Here are two illustrations to explain what I mean.

An editor friend told me about a woman who had published a number of successful books for his publishing house until around 1990. For ten years she didn't write. In early 2000 she sent the house a manuscript. My editor friend said, "It was of the same quality as her previous books. But it wasn't any better." He rejected it.

By contrast, in 2003, I taught at a large conference. The conference director must have been pleased with my presentation, because even though he normally does not schedule the same teachers two years in a row, he invited me back to teach at the 2004 conference. Eight months later, the director e-mailed and said he wondered if I wanted to teach the same course I had already taught or another course.

When I responded, I told him that as soon as he had asked me to teach the following year, I had begun to search for new material and for ways to make my class better.

"You've made my day, and you're a man after my own heart," he responded. "So few keep improving. That's one reason I like having you teach."

My point in telling this is to say that I truly want to be the man with five bags of gold. I want to take every ability God has given me and do everything I can to double or triple it. I don't want to be satisfied with what I was able to do last year or last decade.

As I've pondered that story of the three servants and prayed about that man who started with five bags, I've also been aware of another powerful statement in the story. Here it is again: "Take the money from this servant [the one-bag servant] and give it to the one with the ten bags of gold" (Matthew 25:28, NLT). This time, think about the third servant instead of the one who would soon have eleven bags.

This tells the same as the adage "Use it or lose it." It says that when we faithfully use what we have—no matter how little we may think we have—God honors our faithfulness. And if we keep using those abilities, God adds to them. If we don't use what God has given us, doesn't it imply that the gift will be taken from us?

The best way I can illustrate this from my own experience is to mention learning a language. In the 1990s I went with a group to Nicaragua to build a house for a pastor. I started about a month ahead of time trying to learn as much Spanish as I could. I also memorized a number of Bible verses in the language.

Once we arrived in Nicaragua, I conversed with the nationals. One time in church I gave a lengthy greeting in Spanish. I picked up the words to two hymns and could sing them when I returned home to the United States. But I didn't use my Spanish after that. What little I had—and it was a small amount— was gone within a year or two. I didn't use it, so I lost what I had learned.

Isn't that the way God works in us? No matter how little tal-cnt we have (and we may have more than we think), if we use what God gives us, it increases. Or we lose it through disuse.

I can speak only for myself, but shortly after I realized that God had called me to write, I made a twofold promise. First, I promised I would not stop learning, so that I could continue to grow as a writer. Second, I would help others to become their best as well.

Each day in my prayer time—and I've been doing this for more than twenty years—I pray for God to make me the best writer I can be. If I were a banker, a stockbroker, someone on the assembly line, or a clerk in the hardware department, the prin-ciple would remain the same. God has called us to be faithful with what we have. If we use what we have and—here's the catch—improve on what we have, God will bless and multiply it.

> *I am the five-bag person.*
> *Whatever you give me, help me to use it as I*
> *   continue to grow and improve.*
> *Help me give myself to your service and invest*
> *   my talents in others so they may also grow*
> *   and improve their abilities.*

14

COMPASSIONATE ARMS

lmost everyone knows the parable of the prodigal son. It's a simple story Jesus told (and it's recorded in Luke 15). The point of most parables seems to be to make us uncomfortable—to make the listeners say, "Is that really the way I am?" This one is no different.

Jesus aimed this lesson at religious leaders. Jesus told of a son who asks for his portion of the inheritance, gets it, and wastes everything. When he hits bottom and lives among the pigs, he comes to his senses and returns home.

The son considers begging his father for a lowly job, just to have food to eat. Instead, a loving father welcomes him and prepares a big feast. The older brother (obviously representing the Pharisees) rebukes his father for taking the boy back and (worse) for declaring a feast day. In effect, he says, "You never did that for me, and I've been the good son." The father has to kindly explain to the older brother that he could have had a huge feast anytime.

Yes, it's an open rebuke to the Pharisees of Jesus' day; it's an open rebuke to the Pharisees of our day. As we read the story with modern eyes, we sometimes see ourselves as the younger son. We've blown it, failed God, and gone astray. But when we come to our senses, we return to God.

After we've been members of the Christian community for a few years, we tend to see ourselves as the older brother—if we're honest with ourselves. We've been living the dedicated life, know the standards, and live faithfully. We don't like it when newcomers (a nice way of saying "sinners" or "that son of yours," as the older brother did) come in and receive grace, blessings, honor, and prestige that we secretly believe we deserve for our many years of faithfulness.

In my Christian experience, I've seen myself as the younger son and sometimes (sad to say) as the older son. Quite recently, in thinking through this parable, I began to think of myself as the father.

Yes, I'm aware that the obvious interpretation of the parable is that the father represents God. However, one of the wonderful things about parables is that there are so many different ways of approaching them.

What if I were the father in a story like that? What if I had the opportunity to enrich, bless, and encourage? I would also have the opportunity to depress, curse, and discourage.

Actually, I have the opportunity to do both. I *am* like the father in the story. I can stretch out my arms and embrace sinners like the young son, and I can push away sinners like the self-righteous, older son.

What would it be like, I've asked myself, *if I lived like the father in the story?* It would mean that I would understand grace and dispense it eagerly. And in thinking about grace, I figured out something that's helped me in my daily living: I can only offer as much grace to others as I have received myself.

If, for instance, I understand God's forgiveness—if I have experienced grace that says, "You've been a terrible sinner, but I've wiped away all the evil and wrongdoing"—I know how to respond. I can turn that grace around and offer it to others.

One reason for so little forgiveness in the church today is that we, who need to forgive, don't feel forgiven. We don't realize the immensity of our failures and our need for God's forgiveness. Too few of us have cried out like David, "Don't take your Spirit from me" (see Psalm 51:11).

Another way to say this is that, until we have been broken, we can't understand brokenness in someone else. Let's look at that older brother again. He watches the younger son leave with the money, and later he learns that his brother has returned with tattered clothes and empty hands. He sees only a fallen, despicable man, and he despises him.

Why did the older son react like that? Isn't it possible that's the only way he knew how to respond? If he had been the younger son and had done the despicable things, wouldn't he have condemned himself? Wouldn't he have felt unworthy and undeserving? I think so.

The younger son left with bright smiles and impossibly high hopes; that same son returned with a woeful face and an empty heart. At the end of the story, which son understood forgiveness and grace?

Isn't that how life works—really? We can give only what we have received. We can dispense love only if we've been loved. We can truly offer forgiveness to others only after we've experienced the power of being forgiving.

Perhaps this will help explain what I mean. When I was a pastor in the early 1980s, most ministers in the city wouldn't marry divorced people. If they did, the "innocent" party had to prove the other was guilty of adultery and then the pastor (often with great reluctance) performed the ceremony. One minister named Gene refused to marry divorced people for any reason. "Even if the husband beats her every day," he said to me, "as long as he wants to stay married, she cannot divorce him."

Guess what happened to Gene? Yes, his marriage fell apart after nearly twenty years. He came to see me and cried for a long time as he told me his sad story of his wife walking out. There was no adultery or other horrible sin. "I just don't love you" was all she would say. A week later Gene offered his resignation to the congregation. To their credit, they refused. I suspect they knew more about grace than he did.

I haven't seen Gene for several years, but he has remarried and has become more openly accepting and affirming of hurting people. I've heard that he no longer seeks to distinguish between the innocent and the guilty partner.

I'll also tell you something about myself and the work of grace. Like a lot of Christians, I believed anger was one of the worst sins any Christian could harbor. I worked hard at forgiving and being kind and all those other things. When I lived in Africa, on one occasion I exploded. I could tell the story in a way to justify my actions of yelling and raving. The truth is, one of the Africans touched a vulnerable spot in me—something I didn't want to see about myself. My anger seethed. It took me a long time to live down the experience and to accept a terrible reality about who I was. One day I finally said to God, "I'm an angry person." That may not sound like much, but it was a powerful admission on my part.

I'm not free from anger—the flames of ire erupt occasionally—but two things have happened. First, I know a little more about who I am. Second, because I know and realize God has forgiven me, I can also reach out to those who spew venom and scream. I'll tell you the reason I can do that: I know they're hurting, and anger is one way to cover up our hurt.

Only as we recognize our own weaknesses—and accept them—can we open up to others and forgive their failures. That's the example of the father in this story. We don't know anything about him except, as a friend of mine said, "If he's supposed to be a human father, he's a much evolved one." He meant that the father in the story didn't lecture and he didn't scream. He didn't say, "I knew you'd ruin your life and come crawling back." No, that father understood pain and discouragement, and love prevailed over everything else.

That is the father who rushed down the road to meet the hurting son. Instead of scolding or listening to a lot of wailing words, the father embraced the boy.

"But while he [the younger son] was still a long way off, the father saw him and was filled with compassion for him; he ran to his son, threw his arms around him and kissed him" (Luke 15:20, NIV).

That's the kind of human being I yearn to be.

I am the father who stands with open arms. Help me reach out to those who hurt and need compassion, because I have experienced your compassion.

15

WISE WORDS

My daughter Wanda was in about the fifth grade when she read the *Wizard of Oz* story. She sat down beside me and told me the story (as if I didn't know it) and then said, "But do you know that those three with Dorothy asked for what they already had? The straw man wanted a brain, but he was the one with the ideas. And the lion wanted courage, and he was the bravest of them all. And the tin man wanted a heart, but he was always sweet and kind."

"That's insightful," I said, "and I'll bet many people didn't pick that up." Then I sheepishly admitted that when I read the book, it hadn't occurred to me.

As I have pondered the story, it also makes me wonder if that's not typical of the way life works. That is, how many times do we ask God for the qualities we already have? I don't refer to those things such as assurance of our relationship or strength to resist temptation. I think of the qualities we pray for.

I can recall several instances in prayer groups where I've listened to people pray. I remember my beloved pastor Arthur Dodzweit praying for a tender heart and asking God to make him more loving. He was one of the most loving people I've ever known.

In the same church there was a man named Ozzie, and I often heard him pray for God to open his heart and make him more generous and sensitive to those around him. In our conversations, he thought only of the times when he had failed; I saw him as a generous, openhearted person.

As I mentioned in the story of the "Great Stone Face," is it possible that we tend to pray for gifts we already have? Can it be that we focus on the downside or the less-than-perfect use of our abilities and miss the reality of our giftedness? I wonder if we're attracted to the gifts we already have—in some measure—and yearn for them because they remain unrecognized by us.

I love the story of God appearing to Solomon and infusing him with wisdom. It's a story found in 1 Kings 3. The king, who has only recently succeeded his father, has a dream. The Lord says, "Ask for whatever you want me to give you" (verse 5, NIV).

When Solomon answers, he refers to himself as a little child—not because of his youth, but it's a way of referring to his lack of understanding and naiveté. Here's his request: "I am only a little child and do not know how to carry out my duties. Your servant is here among the people you have chosen, a great people, too numerous to count or number. So give your servant a discerning heart to govern your people and to distinguish between right and wrong" (verses 7–9).

His answer pleases God. "Since you have asked for this and not for long life or wealth for yourself, nor have asked for the death of your enemies but for discernment in administering justice, I will do what you have asked. I will give you a wise and discerning heart, so that there will never have been anyone like you, nor will there ever be" (verses 11, 12). God also adds what Solomon doesn't ask for—riches and honor.

Doesn't that incident show the wisdom of Solomon from the beginning? Wasn't that insightful for him to ask for discernment instead of wealth or long life?

Perhaps that's a powerful lesson to us. It's the same story we find in all kinds of fairy tales and parables. Sixty years ago there was a popular children's book called *The Bluebird.* The family seeks the bird because it's supposed to bring happiness. They leave home and go everywhere searching. They never find the bird, eventually coming home discouraged, and there—at their home—they discover the bluebird they went out into the world to find.

The principle is the same. That which we already have may be the thing we seek the most. Why is that so?

I'm not sure, but I have an idea. Look at Solomon, who wasn't the firstborn of David. He certainly shouldn't have been the one to reign as his father's successor. Didn't God give the king the qualities he needed to be a great king?

Okay, before I go on, people usually rush in and remind us that the wise man came to a bad end. He married foreign women who turned him away from Yahweh and worshiped other gods. Yes, he did foolish things—and that's difficult to grasp.

Those are choices he made, perhaps out of weakness. Or perhaps because he was so brilliant and wise, he stopped learning and opening himself to God. Perhaps he allowed his love for foreign wives to turn his heart away from godly wisdom. I don't know.

If we can move away from the end of his life, however, and focus on the beginning, we see God at work. It's simple. If God calls us to a work, a ministry, or an occupation, and then God equips us for that position, we tend to feel scared and uncertain when we start. Don't we usually begin praying for the ability needed for the task? We may not have all the skills, but I assume that we've already been infused with the gifts we need.

In the matter of wisdom, let's look at that again. When I was in my twenties or even thirties, I didn't pray specifically for wisdom. I asked for guidance in various situations; I asked God to help me understand. As I've grown older, I've increasingly valued wisdom and asked God to grant me deeper understanding.

Is it just possible, I asked myself recently, *that I'm asking for the very thing that God is endowing me with?* To make this clearer, let's try a few other terms besides *wisdom.* I prefer to use words such as *common sense, practicality, discernment.* One version of the Bible has Solomon ask for an "understanding mind."

Regardless of the term we use, I suspect that, for most of us, this is part of the gift of maturing—getting older by our years of being alive. If we're maturing, don't words such as *common sense* and *discernment* fit us? The difference between Solomon and most of us aging souls is that God blessed him when he was young, while we tend to accumulate and grasp understanding through life experiences.

As I've struggled over this matter of wisdom, something my friend David Morgan says has helped. David knows me better than anyone except my wife. When I get worked up over a problem, he says in a gentle way, "You know, there's a spiritual solution to every problem."

That's not an original expression, but it is one well worth repeating. And it's true. It's a word of wisdom that helps me focus my problems on God and seek divine guidance.

For example, a year ago I had an offer to write a book for a man who has been a friend for a dozen years. I gave him a date about ten months ahead when I'd be available. The closer I got to that date, the more I realized that I didn't want to write the book for him. The details aren't important, except to say that I didn't know how to drop out.

"There's a spiritual solution to every problem," David reminded me.

His words—his wise counsel—pushed me to do much soul searching. I finally admitted to myself that I didn't want to disappoint my friend. Even from the beginning, I hadn't wanted to write the book. Finally, I admitted to myself that I had been more worried about displeasing him than I was about whether to do the book.

As I prayed and pondered, the solution seemed obvious: Just tell him exactly how I feel. If he backs away from the relationship, that is his choice.

"I can't write the book," I said. "It just isn't something I want to do."

I prepared myself for a blast of anger and recrimination. To my surprise, my friend understood. Although disappointed, he accepted my answer.

I wish I had the wisdom evidenced by Solomon. I yearn for the brilliance that cuts through all the possibilities and seizes on the sensible solution. Sometimes it happens; however, I want it to happen all the time. I yearn for the commonsense solutions that show God's guidance behind my words. I have some of that—perhaps we all do. I want more.

In the prayer below, I have to confess, I'm hesitant to use the word *wisdom.* Maybe it's because it feels like something far beyond my grasp or too brilliant for me to attain. When I substituted *common sense* or *understanding*, it felt easier for me to pray. I've learned, however, that the harder prayers are for me to repeat, the more I need to pray them.

Yes, I yearn for wisdom. I want to be infused with divine common sense and powerful discernment.

I am Solomon.
Please fill me with wisdom.
Help me discern spiritual solutions for every
*   problem.*
Thank you for this gift of understanding.

16

FROM FAILURE TO RESTORATION

How would it feel to be given the chance to travel with a ministry leader you admired greatly? To become part of that person's entourage and learn the work while being with such a person? That has to be a high point in your life.

But what happens if you fail? You get discouraged or you realize that the great person wasn't really so great. Maybe you overvalued the ability of the leader. Perhaps that boss pushed you too hard or had such a surly disposition you couldn't work with him any longer. Or maybe you saw your own weaknesses or your inability to do the task. Is it possible that the position you longed for demanded more commitment than you were able to give?

So you walked away. That must have been a difficult decision even though you knew it was the right thing to do at that time. Or did you? Were you so caught up in needing to get away from the despicable leader that you didn't care whether anyone agreed with you? You couldn't take it any longer. "Anything is better than a life like this."

Another factor was that if you left you would not only feel you had let yourself down, but also you'd fail the people who helped you get that desired position. How will the leader feel? How about your family? Are you letting them down as well?

But you can't take the verbal abuse, or maybe it's the demeaning language or the demanding voice of the leader. You can't think of life being any more miserable than it is right now.

So you quit and you're on your own. And it feels good to be free of the tyrannical, demanding voice of your former hero. Now you are finally free to be yourself and to do whatever you wanted.

Push forward six months. You've been away from the situation long enough, thought about everything objectively, and figured out that you made a mistake. Maybe you were too set in your ways. Maybe you weren't able to bow to anyone else in authority. Anyway, you ran.

That's the story of John Mark. He was the nephew of Barnabas (although some translators use the word "cousin"), and it was because of that great man that John Mark was able to go on what we call the first missionary journey. It's a historic trip. It begins when Barnabas and Saul (Paul) leave Antioch in Syria to proclaim the good news as they travel across Asia Minor. Luke recounts their journeys, and of their first stop on the island of Cyprus he writes, "They proclaimed the word of God in the Jewish synagogues." Then Luke adds, almost as an afterthought, "John was with them as their helper" (Acts 13:5, NIV).

On Cyprus, Paul confronts a false prophet named Bar-Jesus, blinding the man, and the proconsul is amazed. The next verse reads, "From Paphos, Paul and his companions sailed to Perga in Pamphylia, where John left them to return to Jerusalem" (verse 13). No explanation or reason for John's departure is given. If that were the end of the story, readers might assume he had gone on an errand or went to preach there.

We don't hear of John Mark again until after Paul and Barnabas have completed their journey and returned to Syria. When the two men plan for their next trip, we learn a little about the problem. Luke records, "Barnabas wanted to take John, also called Mark, with them, but Paul did not think it wise to take him, because he had deserted them in Pamphylia and had not continued with them in the work" (15:37, 38, NIV).

The author calls it desertion. Perhaps in God's eyes, that's exactly what it was. But to John Mark, it may not have been desertion as much as failure to measure up, the inability to stand up in tough times, or his unwillingness to work under Paul's demands.

Something happened to John Mark—even though we don't know any details—and he left. A year or so later he wants to go again. The problem is, Paul doesn't want him.

Now the young man is faced not only with failure but also feelings of rejection, and he probably struggles with a lack of self-worth. No matter how much he has changed, Paul still won't take him. I can only imagine that John Mark must have thought of the drastic change in Paul, who went out to kill Christians, met Christ on the Damascus road, was converted, with no one but Barnabas standing up for him. Given Paul's own record of change, his reaction to Mark doesn't reflect well on Paul, of course.

But we don't want to just drop John Mark. We don't know everything, and although this is guesswork, it seems obvious that somewhere the young man faced himself, returned, and was ready to make amends and try it again. When Paul said no, here's what happened: "They [Paul and Barnabas] had such a sharp disagreement that they parted company. Barnabas took Mark and sailed for Cyprus, but Paul chose Silas and left" (Acts 15:39, 40, NIV). This is the last mention of Barnabas in the Bible.

It's not the last reference to John Mark.

He is mentioned twice more in the New Testament—and that's what makes him such a hero for me. One mention occurs at the end of Paul's letter to the church at Colosse. "My fellow prisoner Aristarchus sends you his greetings, as does Mark, the cousin of Barnabas. (You have received instructions about him; if he comes to you welcome him)" (Colossians 4:10, TNIV).

We don't know when Paul wrote that letter, but he was in prison, probably in Rome. If that's the case, this was after Paul had made three journeys. Somewhere during the time after John Mark's aborted journey, he and Paul reconciled.

The most powerful statement about the young man, however, appears as one of Paul's last statements to Timothy—and probably his last written letter. He gives Timothy a number of final instructions and says, "Get Mark and bring him with you, because he is helpful to me in my ministry" (2 Timothy 4:11, TNIV).

Here's why I admire John Mark and include him as one of the people I want to imitate. He was wrong—dreadfully wrong. He failed. He turned his back on the ministry and on an opportunity to serve God (although he may have seen himself only as freeing himself from Paul).

The point is that the young man made a serious mistake. Barnabas apparently accepted him and forgave him. Not only was he the young man's uncle (or cousin), but as I show elsewhere, this is typical of my hero Barnabas.

Let's focus on John Mark. It must have been a totally shameful time for him when he walked away from Paul and Barnabas. The guilt he struggled with had to be enormous. Perhaps he felt self-loathing and a sense of worthlessness.

I suspect that most of us have had similar feelings. Our situations weren't like John Mark's, but we've tasted the bitterness of failure. My failures have come largely over my anger—blowing up at someone, acts of harshness, and times of mean temperedness. Once we speak (or scream) the words, we can't put them back inside.

Yes, I've been on the guilty side of that situation many times. More than once I've wept and cried for God to forgive me. I also struggle even more with forgiving myself. Many times I've heard myself crying out, "After all these years of being a Christian, and still I . . ."

I like John Mark. I also admire him because he was able to humble himself and go back—and even more, he redeemed himself. Paul broke down eventually. Even the one who didn't think it wise to take him had to admit that John Mark had redeemed himself.

Yes, I like John Mark. He was wrong and he was willing to do whatever it took to make it right. That is, he was willing to say words such as "I'm sorry" or "I made a serious mistake" or even "I sinned." He went back and started again.

That's an important point—he went back and started again. He didn't just pass it off with "Oh, well, that's over, and I'm forgiven." I believe it was the going back that brought about Paul's commendation of him.

I want to make a point of this because of something my wife struggled with for years. Shirley can't remember when she didn't believe—she's one of those cradle Christians. Along the way, she made a few mistakes (she is human) but never turned away from God or was involved in any moral failure. But she felt her failures just as deeply as if they had been moral lapses.

In the midst of that struggle to get straightened out, she heard a pastor say, "If you ever fail and go astray, you can never be as close to God as you were before." For years she believed what he had said and moaned because she couldn't have that relationship she had once cherished.

She told me that story a few months after we married, and I was horrified that she had accepted the man's word without question. "I think it's exactly the opposite. You have now known grace. You understand what it feels like to fail and to be forgiven. You're stronger and more committed now than you've ever been. You know—by experience—a deeper sense of God's unconditional love."

Shirley grasped that.

I suspect John Mark did too. He had failed, but he didn't remain a failure. He grew from it and served Jesus Christ. By the time Paul was an old man, he had learned to think of John Mark not only as one of his followers but also as a profitable disciple.

> *I am John Mark.*
> *I have failed and made mistakes.*
> *I am also forgiven and I am loved.*
> *Remind me that when I confess my failure, you*
> *forgive me and make me stronger for the*
> *next test.*

17

No Small Tasks

I remember when channeling and past lives first hit the TV talk shows and pop magazines. In the early days, everyone who I heard claiming to remember past lives had once been someone famous. I don't believe in past lives, but my point isn't to debate the issue. What struck me was that connection with the famous personages of history. Maybe there's something in most of us that wants to be famous or special to the world.

When I was a seminary student, one of my classmates commented that he didn't want to accept a call to a small church. "I'm much better preaching to a large crowd than to a small one."

About the same time, representatives from rural Appalachia came to visit the seminary. They offered to help students with a large grant to enable them to finish their education. In return, the students would have to agree to become pastors to two or more small churches. They called them "yoked ministries." So far as I know, they didn't get one serious applicant. "Who wants to bury himself in the backwoods?" one of my classmates said to me.

Here's another story from my past. The editor of a publishing house asked me to befriend a new writer. "I think he has potential," the editor said. "Maybe you could encourage him and nudge him along."

I called the man, and we met for lunch. "I see so much drivel out there," he said almost as the first sentence. "I want to write classics. I want to write books that will endure."

"Do you think people intentionally write bad books?" I asked.

"I won't publish anything unless I know it's going to endure," he said as if he hadn't heard my question. For several minutes he railed about people writing "fluff and empty words" and affirmed he would never be involved in such futility.

We never met after that luncheon. He made it clear that he didn't need help to write the great Christian books that God had destined him to produce. For the next decade I watched for books by him. So far as I know, he has never published.

Now I want to point to a biblical account. On the night of Jesus' betrayal, he met with his twelve disciples in an upper room. John 13 contains the insightful account that enables us to grasp the disciples in more human terms.

In homes with slaves, the lowest of them would greet guests, help them loosen their sandals, and provide water and a basin to wash their feet before the guests walked into the house. On that night, none of the twelve volunteered to wash feet.

Who would want such a demeaning task? Those same men had previously argued among themselves over who would be greatest in Jesus' kingdom. James and John had their mother beg on their behalf for positions one and two.

At the Thursday evening meal they're still the same men. "So he [Jesus] got up from the meal, took off his outer clothing, and wrapped a towel around his waist. After that, he poured water into a basin and began to wash his disciples' feet, drying them with the towel that was wrapped around him" (John 13:4, NIV). Apparently none of them objected until Peter finally asked Jesus why he was doing such a lowly task. The implication, of course, was that "one of them" (not Peter, of course) should have done that dirty, demeaning job.

These illustrations point out a prevalence in our culture—perhaps in all cultures. We want the top positions. How many of us willingly accept ourselves as mediocre? How many of us, given the choice, would take the obscure and insignificant position rather than reach for the starring role?

This isn't against ambition or meant to stifle anyone's desire for self-improvement. It is a way of pointing out that maybe we have our priorities mixed up. Maybe we need to start small and let our work speak for itself.

Here it is in the positive form: For godly people, there are no small tasks. Every task is important. Paul says it this way when he addresses Christian slaves. He exhorts them to obey their masters with deep respect. "Work hard, but not just to please your masters when they are watching. As slaves of Christ, do the will of God with all your heart. Work with enthusiasm, as though you were working for the Lord rather than for people" (Ephesians 6:6, 7, NLT).

One of the best examples of this attitude in action is Stephen. We know him primarily as the first martyr of the Christian faith. Most of Acts 7 is a bold, magnificent sermon given by Stephen just before his accusers kill him. He never finishes the message, because the enraged Jewish leaders shake their fists and stone him. Luke adds this: "But Stephen, full of the Holy Spirit, gazed steadily upward into heaven" (verse 55, NLT).

"Full of the Holy Spirit" is an interesting phrase, and it's the second time it's used to refer to Stephen.

For background, recall that the church started in Jerusalem. The apostles and early believers met regularly on a communal basis by sharing everything with each other. We understand that all of them shared duties, no matter how menial they seemed. But problems arose when Greek-speaking widows felt discriminated against in the daily distribution of food.

The apostles called the believers together for a kind of council meeting. They made it clear that they believed God wanted them to preach and teach the Word of God instead of administer a food program. "Now look around among yourselves, brothers, and select seven men who are well respected and are full of the Holy Spirit and wisdom. We will put them in charge of this business" (Acts 6:3, 4, NLT).

Those seven men started with the lowest jobs—just as Jesus had done on the night of the Passover when he washed dirty feet. After he washed their feet, he said, "Since I, the Lord and Teacher, have washed your feet, you ought to wash each other's feet. I have given you an example to follow. Do as I have done to you. How true it is that a servant is not greater than the master" (John 13:14–16, NLT).

Jesus set the example for us. Which of us follow that model?

Stephen is my personal nomination. I could also have mentioned Philip. Acts 8 contains two wonderful accounts of his ministry. Like Stephen, Philip waited on tables. He and six other men did the humiliating work of serving others. I'm sure they had to contend with grumbling and perhaps even derisive remarks, but they did what there was for them to do.

Stephen, who served others, becomes the first martyr. But he becomes that martyr as a result of his vigorous preaching, holy boldness, and godly commitment.

One of the first times I read the story about choosing seven men of integrity and full of the Holy Spirit, it amazed me. Why such lofty qualifications for such a nothing kind of job? Perhaps they had to choose respected men, but why that other part about being full of the Holy Spirit? I would probably have chosen people who weren't good at doing anything else.

Is it possible that it takes that kind of fullness of the Spirit to be able to do the no-glory jobs—the kind that no one sees or notices?

One experience helps me realize how difficult it is to take the lowly position. During my final year of college, the president of the college asked me to travel for six weeks with a men's quartet, visit churches and organizations, and tell them about the school. He didn't designate a leader, and that caused some friction.

By the second week, the bickering among us was terrible. We had one rental car, and each of us wanted to drive or at least sit in the front seat. Often we stayed in homes, and each of us wanted the best accommodations. We didn't like the way the others drove. We grumbled because we didn't stop often enough or because we stopped too often or were off the road too long to eat or didn't relax enough before we got back into the car.

By the third week, I felt heartsick and wondered why I had agreed to be part of the group. I wasn't any better than the other four and had become just as petty. One night an argument broke out and all five us—limited to one large motel room—went to bed upset at the others.

I lay in bed for perhaps an hour. After I grumbled to God about their failures and shortcomings, I still couldn't sleep. I finally realized that I was as wrong as they were. (That took perhaps another half hour.)

"Forgive me," I cried out. I realized the major problem was that each of us wanted to be in charge. Each of us felt we could do a better job of leading the group than the others.

As I tossed in bed, I realized that I had to change. I didn't know what to do or how to make up for my bad behavior. As I lay there, I had a thought. I got up, went to each bed, and picked up the others' shoes and carried them into the bathroom. I spent the next twenty minutes polishing five pairs of shoes. It wasn't quite like washing feet, but it was the best I could come up with.

I'm not sure any of the others noticed I had polished their shoes, and that didn't matter. I had done this as an act of contrition to God.

At breakfast I apologized to the group. "I'm sorry for wanting to run things," I said. One by one, the others admitted similar feelings.

I don't remember if we elected one of us to lead or if we simply learned to work better with each other. I do know that, for me at least, it no longer mattered where I sat in the car. I could opt for the bed the others didn't want. I could do that simply because God had dealt with me and the bed didn't matter.

That's the point: It no longer mattered. I was there to be one of the group and not to be in charge.

At the end of the six weeks, we parted with big hugs and warm smiles. "It's been a good time," one of them said.

It *had* been a good time—and a powerful learning experience for me. It wasn't easy for me to acknowledge that God hadn't called me to correct my classmates' behavior or to smugly assert my superiority.

I wish I could add that since that date I've always been willing and eager to take the lesser places or seek obscure positions. Perhaps the reason that experience stands out is that it was a standout experience. That event showed me how I could be different. It gave me something to work toward in my maturing experience.

Was it Stephen's faithfulness in serving food that brought him into a higher position? We have no way of knowing, but I don't think so. I suspect that from the beginning Stephen had shown himself as faithful, hardworking, and committed. When the people needed seven men, he was a natural choice to be one of them. He started out with the small tasks, and the day came when God gave him greater responsibilities.

I want to be like Stephen. I want to commit myself to whatever is at hand for me to do, regardless of how small or insignificant the task may be. I want to wait tables, change tires, pick up garbage, or do whatever I can to be faithful to God and helpful to others.

> *I am Stephen, the man who sought no big*
> *position.*
> *May I rejoice in whatever task you give me and*
> *enjoy whatever place you put me in.*
> *Whatever task I have, may I faithfully do it to*
> *please you, O God.*

18

PERSISTENT VOICE

Hannah is one of those little-known but greatly admired women in the Old Testament. I admire her too. The story about Hannah that I relate to is how she became Samuel's mother.

She was one of two wives of a man named Elkanah. The other wife, Peninnah, bore children, but Hannah didn't. As we might expect, Peninnah makes fun of the barren wife. Elkanah, however, loves Hannah very much and favors her. That probably provokes the other wife even more. "Hannah would finally be reduced to tears and would not even eat" (1 Samuel 1:7, NLT).

In those days, the tabernacle was at Shiloh. Like all good Jews of the day, Elkanah and his family go there for the three annual feasts. One year a heavyhearted Hannah goes into the tabernacle to pray for a son. Apparently she exhibits such anguish that she attracts the attention of Eli the high priest. The Bible says, "Hannah was in deep anguish, crying bitterly" (verse 10) as she prayed. She told God that if she had a son, she would dedicate him to God. She and her husband were of the priestly line, and that meant he would become a lifetime priest. He was apparently also dedicated as a Nazirite.[9]

Eli, however, watches her carefully. "Seeing her lips moving but hearing no sound, he thought she had been drinking" (verse 13). Hannah denies that charge, of course, and tells him that she was opening her heart to God "out of great anguish and sorrow" (verse 16).

The priest then says, "Cheer up! May the God of Israel grant the request you have asked of him" (verse 17).

"'Oh, thank you, sir!' she exclaimed. Then she went back and began to eat again, and she was no longer sad" (verse 18).

The family returns home from the feast, and Hannah conceives and gives birth to a son she names Samuel (which means "asked of God").

That's a simple, straightforward tale of answered prayer. But it's more than a story of answered prayer—it's also a story of prevailing prayer.

Prevailing prayer. I don't hear that term used much these days. In earlier days I also heard the idea referred to as holding on to the horns of the altar. That term refers to the story of Adonijah, who tried to wrest the throne from his half-brother Solomon. When he failed, the Bible records, "Adonijah himself was afraid of Solomon, so he rushed to the sacred tent and caught hold of the horns of the altar" (1 Kings 1:50, NLT). This was a symbolic way of pleading for mercy—a kind of last resort.

---

9. *The word* Nazirite *means "separated" or "consecrated." Nazirites were separated from common pleasures of life and could not shave their heads as long as they kept that vow. A few, such as Samuel and Samson, were dedicated as life-long Nazirites. See Numbers 6 for a biblical explanation.*

"So King Solomon summoned Adonijah, and they brought him down from the altar. . . . And Solomon dismissed him, saying, 'Go on home'" (verse 53).

Another term I rarely hear today is what people once called "praying through." By that they meant that they would persist in prayer until they broke through every barrier and reached heaven (that is, until they felt assured that God would give them an answer).

We also used to speak of *importuning prayer,* after a parable Jesus recorded in Luke 11:5–13. The story is simple: A visitor comes at night and the householder has no food. In ancient cultures, the most insulting and most inhospitable act was for you to refuse to feed someone who came to visit. So in desperation the host races through the neighborhood, begging food for his visitor.

Jesus concludes, "So I tell you, keep on asking, and you will be given what you ask for. Keep on looking, and you will find. Keep on knocking, and the door will be opened" (verse 9, NLT).

The principle of prevailing prayer is a strong one in the Bible, even though it has lost favor in modern times. Instead of persevering in prayer, many tell God one time and then repeat the words of Jesus: "Yet not my will, but yours be done" (Luke 22:42, TNIV). They pray those words as if to say, "There is nothing more to pray."

They don't seem to realize that Jesus said those words after a prolonged period of agony. He began by pleading with the Father not to make him die. When he finally surrendered, those were his words—but they came as a result of intense, earnest pleading with God. Hannah would never have stopped after a single petition. Sometimes our burdens become so heavy that it's as if we can do nothing but pray and continue to pray until we feel peace.

~

Let's go back to Hannah. What strong, powerful yearning that woman must have had. Not only the constant torment and ridicule of Peninnah, but also she suffered the ridicule of the culture. Worse, she must have felt worthless. No matter how much Elkanah loved her, she must have felt inadequate for being barren and unable to give her husband a child.

For us, the principle isn't about barrenness but about the deep longings in our hearts. We pray because we have no peace until we "pray through" and feel God lifting the burden.

Here's how I learned about prevailing prayer. About a year after I became a believer, I frequently thought of other members of my family. Over a period of two years, my heart felt heavy because I had peace with God, but my dad and my siblings didn't. I wanted them to experience God's love for themselves. One night I couldn't sleep, and I got up around midnight. I determined to spend the entire night in prayer if necessary, but I wouldn't stop praying until God assured me of their salvation.

I have no idea how long I prayed—perhaps two hours, although it may have been longer—but I stopped only after a peaceful assurance filled my heart that they would turn to Christ. It took years, but eventually all of them professed faith in Christ.

Here's one other experience of prevailing prayer. The mission board sent Shirley and me to a remote area of Kenya near

Lake Victoria called South Nyanza. After about seven months, we realized that nothing much happened no matter how much we prayed, taught, or preached. We had a lot of dissension in our midst. I was part of the problem, because I had made a number of mistakes. Even though I could excuse myself because of my ignorance, I knew I had been wrong. I confessed my failures to God and asked the people I had offended to forgive me.

Still we witnessed no visible results. In desperation I asked my wife and three Africans to join me every morning at six o'clock to pray. First, we went through a protracted period of searching our hearts and asking God's forgiveness. Then we pleaded for harmony and for spiritual awakening in our area.

When we started, the five of us agreed we would prevail in prayer every morning for at least a year, longer if we had to. Although we kept our commitment to pray for a year, about two months passed before God started to answer.

People in areas we had not been able to get into before came to us and asked us to start a church in their "location" (like our county). In Kadem Location, we started a church, and more than two hundred people turned to Christ. One man complained to the chief (much like our sheriff) and asked him to close the church. The chief said, "You look at those people. Those are men who never paid their poll taxes, but they pay them now. I know several who were drunkards, but they no longer drink." He listed other differences and added, "So why would I want to stop the church? They make my job easier."

Within a year, we had started fifty churches. God had answered our prevailing prayer.

This great awakening happened because we felt a burden and refused to simply say, "God will do whatever needs to be done." We felt the urgency and the burning desire to pray for God to use us to reach people—maybe the kind of intensity Hannah felt when she prayed for a son. We held on to the horns of the altar and refused to let go until we knew God had heard us. Finally, like Hannah, we saw the results. We had honored God by our prevailing prayer.

That's my lesson from this delightful story about Hannah. I can say it in three simple statements: First, she knew her need. Second, she knew that only God could provide the answer. Third, she did the one thing she could do: she prayed and refused to stop until she believed God had heard her.

Yes, I like Hannah. She's an example to me. A woman barren for many years finally cries out, and a loving, compassionate God hears her prayers. Sometimes the answer may be the words of Jesus "Not my will," but we can't know that unless we do what both Hannah and Jesus did—pray fervently, passionately, and with a commitment to prevail until we have an answer.

> *I am Hannah.*
> *Help me realize my needs, and acknowledge you*
> *are the only one who can provide.*
> *I pray passionately and committedly for you*
> *to answer.*

19

PUZZLING LEADERSHIP

Matt was one of the most fascinating men I've ever known. I've seldom met anyone who had the vision for reaching people for God the way he did. I've seldom met anyone more zealous or committed.

We served together as missionaries in Africa. He seemed always three steps ahead of the rest of us in strategies and methods. No matter what he tried, his methods worked. He had the ability to see ahead, figure out the problems in advance, present solutions, and then offer a workable plan. The rest of us hadn't even thought of starting such an action before he had it worked out.

Matt had another side too. He belittled others or held up minor mistakes (such as embarrassing someone for mispronouncing a Swahili word). He rebuked people in public about things that should have been handled in private.

I could make a lengthy list of all his failures, yet I admired him. It wasn't his vision or his marvelous ability but his sensitivity that I admired. It may seem odd to use a word like "sensitivity" when I've already portrayed him as highly insensitive. Yet both were true.

When it came to Matt's relationship with God, that's when I saw a side of him that I admired. For example, one time a group of us missionaries met for a three-day retreat. The first night, one of the men called Matt on his behavior and told all of us what Matt had done.

While he talked, I saw the shock in Matt's eyes. When the accusation ended, he asked, "Did I do that to you? I had no idea."

Three of us who had witnessed the action affirmed that the accusation was true.

Tears slid down Matt's cheeks, and he buried his head. Right in front of at least forty people, Matt dropped to his knees and silently cried to God for forgiveness while the rest of us stared at him. A few minutes later, Matt came over to us and asked us to forgive him. Without any doubt, I believe his repentance was totally genuine.

That was the pattern I saw with Matt over the next few years. He remained as difficult as ever. (He didn't know it, but the Africans referred to him as Hammerhead. By that they meant he was as stubborn and hard as the iron head of a hammer.) But once in a while God convicted him of wrongdoing, such as speaking a harsh word or doing something unkind. When confronted, Matt quickly asked forgiveness and cried out to God. More than once, I watched him leave a meeting and go to a private place and pray for an extended period of time.

Matt died a couple of years ago, and so far as I know, he remained an enigma until the end. I disliked the way he pushed people around, but I admired the sensitivity of his soul when facing God.

Matt reminds me of how I see David in the Bible. He was a great king and he built up the kingdom of Israel. As a warrior, he led the armies in defeating all their enemies. He's referred to in Scripture as a man after God's own heart. He wrote some of the deepest, most tender psalms that appear in the Bible.

On the other hand, he committed adultery with a woman and had her husband murdered in battle to cover his shameful crime. He apparently didn't do a very good job of raising his children. Two of them tried to rip the kingdom from him, and one actually succeeded for a while.

David was an enigma: a puzzling, ambiguous, and inexplicable individual. He could be ruthless and he could be tender. I want to focus on the tender side of the man. That's the part of David I want to imitate.

Here are a few of the reasons.

David had a great capacity for friendship. Think about Jonathan and David, who together produced one of the supreme examples of male bonding. David formed a friendship with King Saul's son—the heir apparent—even though both men knew David would become the next king instead of Jonathan. Their powerful relationship transcended that huge obstacle.

David responded to the tender tugs of the Holy Spirit. When confronted by the prophet Nathan over his sin with Bathsheba, he broke down. He offered no defense for his actions. Later, after the child was born and was dying, this is the man who refused to wash, shave, or eat. Instead, he prayed for God to have mercy on that child, and he continued to pray until the infant died.

David forgave those who wronged him. After the death of Absalom, who had deposed him, I'm not sure what emotion I would have expected in him. Sadness perhaps, but also peace and satisfaction because he was back on the throne. Instead, he wept until Joab, the commander of the army, warned him that if he didn't stop grieving he'd lose all his support.

David honored the position of the king and saw it as an appointment by God. This is the man who had several opportunities to kill Saul when the king and his men hunted him as a fugitive. He refused and said, "This is the Lord's anointed." What sensitivity to God! Despite his shrewdness and ruthlessness, David would never do anything personally to depose the king.

For example, King Saul constantly tried to kill David because he knew that if the younger man lived he would become king. On one occasion Saul went into a cave to relieve himself, and David, hiding in the cave, cut off part of the king's coat. "Afterward, David was conscience-stricken for having cut off a corner of his [Saul's] robe. He said to his men, 'The LORD forbid that I should do such a thing to my master, the LORD's anointed, or lift my hand against him; for he is the anointed of the LORD'" (1 Samuel 24:5, 6, NIV).

After Saul left the cave, from a distance "David bowed down and prostrated himself with his face to the ground" (verse 8). He held up the cloth and pointed out that he could have killed the king, but Saul could now see that he had been delivered by God. "May the LORD judge between you and me. And may the LORD avenge the wrongs you have done to me, but my hand will not touch you" (verse 12).

This shows the true heart of David. We see his soul more fully through his writings. He probably wrote Psalm 23, and we associate Psalm 51 with his repentance after his affair with Bathsheba.

The verse that has struck me as the most powerful in the latter psalm is verse 4:

Against you, you only, have I sinned and done what is
    evil in your sight. (NIV)

It's not that David overlooked his sins against people, but
he saw failure in its ultimate place. All wrong behavior is finally
against God. We hurt people and we cause heartaches and problems, but all sin starts and ends as an act against God's laws.

This is the side of the flawed man that intrigues me the
most. He saw his evil ways not as mistakes or miscalcula-
tions but as acts directed against God. In that same psalm he
prayed,

Do not cast me from your presence or take your Holy
    Spirit from me. (verse 11, NIV)

Those words flow from a contrite, repenting heart. Such
expressions not only endear David to me but also make me
yearn for that sensitivity to God's ultimate aims and purposes.

Too often in my life I feel as if God has to write the words in
twelve-foot-high letters for me to grasp my failures or sins. I
even have difficulty using the word *sin*. I like words such as *mistake* and *error*, and I want to excuse myself because I've had a
bad day or I'm in a foul mood. Not David.

Have mercy on me, O God, according to your
    unfailing love; according to your great compassion
    blot out my transgression. (verse 1, NIV)

A person who prays that way understands grace and forgiveness. This is the person who hears God's whisper and responds

with "Yes, I am the man." This is not only a man after God's own heart; he is also a man after my heart.

> *I am David.*
> *I have failed more times than anyone can count,*
> *but you have also given me a tender heart*
> *and sensitivity to your Spirit.*
> *Thank you for that sensitivity to hear you point*
> *out my failures.*
> *Thank you for giving me the ability to hear,*
> *repent, and rejoice in your compassion.*

20

A GIFT OF GRACE

Most people don't even know who Mephibosheth was; others might wonder why I chose him for inclusion in this book.

He was the grandson of King Saul, David's fiercest enemy, and he was the only son of Jonathan, David's best friend. He also survived the purging of Saul's family after David ascended to the throne. In those days, when a new king came into power, one of his first official acts was to kill every pretender to the throne. David left no one alive who could have any kind of claim to the throne by reason of birth. The only remaining offspring was Mephibosheth, who was lame.

When Saul first tried to kill his eventual successor, his own son Jonathan pleaded with David, "Do not ever cut off your kindness from my family—even when the LORD has cut off every one of David's enemies from the face of the earth" (1 Samuel 20:15, NIV). David promised Jonathan he would not.

Later, when Saul seems to realize that David will ultimately prevail, he pleads,

"Now swear to me by the LORD that you will not cut off my descendants or wipe out my name from my father's family."

So David gave his oath to Saul. (1 Samuel 24:21, 22, NIV)

Years after David ascended the throne, he remembered his promise and asked, "Is there anyone still left of the house of Saul to whom I can show kindness for Jonathan's sake?" (2 Samuel 9:1, NIV). The words translated show that "kindness" isn't quite the meaning of the Hebrew phrase. The Hebrew also includes the idea of loyalty, and this reflects the covenant David and Jonathan made together.

David calls in Mephibosheth, who has been crippled since childhood and is unable to walk. The king promises, "I will restore to you all the land that belonged to your grandfather Saul, and you will always eat at my table" (9:7, NIV).

Mephibosheth's response is one of gratefulness.

Some have suggested that David conferred that honor on the man so he could watch him, but there seems no evidence to support that idea. Because he was crippled, that would make him unacceptable as a king or leader. Mephibosheth could easily have been put to death. Besides, years had passed since the death of Saul. No one would have pressed David to remember the promise he made to his friend.

Later, when David's son Absalom makes himself king of Israel, David and all his loyal friends flee Jerusalem. Mephibosheth doesn't run away with the king. But when David returns in triumph, Ziba, Mephibosheth's servant, tells King David that his master stayed "because he thinks, 'Today the house of Israel will give me back my grandfather's kingdom'" (2 Samuel 16:3, NIV).

Ziba is probably lying, and the Bible contains no evidence before or later to support his charge. It's also absurd to think that Absalom, David's ruthless son, would have done anything to elevate anyone from Saul's family. In fact, he would have been more likely to kill Saul's grandson rather than leave the slightest question that the man might rise up and try to wrest the kingdom from Absalom.

Here's how the Bible describes the scene when David returns to Jerusalem and people flock to praise his triumph: "Mephibosheth . . . also went down to meet the king. He had not taken care of his feet or trimmed his mustache or washed his clothes from the day the king left until the day he returned" (2 Samuel 19:24, NIV). He explains to David that Ziba lied about him.

The story as told implies that the biblical writer believed Mephibosheth, but we're not sure David did. (When Ziba lied, David gave him all Mephibosheth's holdings. Now he splits everything between the two men. See 19:24ff.) This was probably done for expediency.

That's the story, and there's just one more reference to the crippled man: "The king [David] spared Mephibosheth son of Jonathan, the son of Saul, because of the oath before the LORD between David and Jonathan son of Saul" (2 Samuel 21:7, NIV). Then it goes on to say that David had the seven sons of Rizpah, one of Saul's concubines, seized and his soldiers killed them. As a male heir of Jonathan or Saul, that left only Mephibosheth.

I want to explain the reason I've chosen Mephibosheth as one of my flawed heroes. He makes me focus on grace.

I'm a zealous Christian. Since my conversion, I've always been heavily involved in the church and working for God. I've loved reaching out and serving Jesus Christ and people. That's also where my problem comes in. At times I'm tempted to remind God of how worthwhile, honorable, and deserving I am. I'm especially prone to that temptation when I want something badly. As a way to bolster my plea and to make the Lord know that I deserve what I ask for, I remind him of my faithfulness.

That's stating it poorly perhaps, but I've been guilty of that kind of thinking many times in my Christian experience. By reminding God of my faithfulness and commitment, I don't have to focus on the reality of grace.

Grace has nothing directly to do with achievement and spiritual productivity. I say "nothing directly" because I believe in an indirect connection. I don't work hard for God in order to receive. Rather, because I have received so much, I work hard in appreciation.

That is, when I'm at my best, grace comes first and then my service. In my worst moments, I reverse the situation.

When David first accepts Mephibosheth, the crippled man gratefully accepts the king's undeserved kindness (which is grace). He finds a place reserved for him every day to eat at the king's table. That means he sits and eats among the royalty. That's rather amazing and is something we find nowhere else in Scripture. In all other instances, kings destroy anyone who might have any claim—no matter how small. Also, no crippled person was ever allowed in the king's palace.

This is the height of grace in the Old Testament. David owes Mephibosheth nothing. True, he had made a vow to Jonathan and to Saul, but he could easily have overlooked such promises—and did for several years after he ascended to the throne. But one day the king wants to show mercy. He reaches out to the undeserving. He extends grace.

That's the way I need to think of my relationship to God. God owes me nothing. When I objectively look at my good and noble deeds, I often admit that I did them with a jaundiced eye. That is, I sometimes did the right thing for impure motives. I did good for others because deep within me was the sense that God would smile on me for my efforts. Or it was a way to manipulate others into liking me or doing me a bigger favor than I did them.

I'm reminded of a little joke between my wife and me. In our early years of marriage, I would do something like set the table or make a telephone call for her.

"That was thoughtful of you," she said the first time.

"Yes, I agree with you."

"Now you've spoiled it," Shirley answered.

Since then, on many occasions, my wife will say, "That was a nice thing to do and, yes, you thought so too."

Although it has become our private joke, I realize that I've actually done nice or kind things to score points in heaven. Maybe my motives will also have some mixture of selflessness and selfishness in them.

Praying as if I'm Mephibosheth helps me in combating that tendency. When I think of David's reaching out to him, I'm able to focus on grace.

He owed his life to David.

He owed his comfort to the king.

He owed his allegiance to his father's best friend.

The undeserving showed his loving gratefulness by refusing to shave, bathe, or dress his wounded feet. I like Mephibosheth.

I wish I could always come to God with that guilelessness and utter vulnerability that says, "Everything I have, including my life, is your gift to me."

> *I am Mephibosheth.*
> *I deserve nothing, but you have given me much.*
> *I rely on your grace and generous love.*
> *And I'm thankful.*

21

A HELPER IN NEED

I wish Paul the apostle had told us more about Onesiphorus. He mentions him only twice in his second letter to Timothy. In the second reference, 2 Timothy 4:19 merely says, "Greet Priscilla and Aquila and the household of Onesiphorus" (NIV).

What intrigues me is the first reference—and it only hints about the man. "May the Lord show mercy to the household of Onesiphorus, because he often refreshed me and was not ashamed of my chains. On the contrary, when he was in Rome, he searched hard for me until he found me. May the Lord grant that he will find mercy from the Lord on that day! You know very well in how many ways he helped me in Ephesus" (2 Timothy 1:16–18, NIV).

In the verses quoted above, Paul laments about those who have turned away from him in his need. "You know that everyone in the province of Asia has deserted me, including Phygelus and Hermogenes" (verse 15). When Paul refers to Asia, he doesn't mean the continent of Asia as we think about it but rather the western part of Asia Minor with its capital at Ephesus—the home of Onesiphorus. That's where Paul had been imprisoned.

Perhaps one reason the tribute of Onesiphorus touches me is because of something I witnessed in the 1980s while I was still a pastor. I was on the council of elders of the Presbytery of Greater Atlanta, a body that oversaw 106 churches. During my second year on that council, one incident greatly disturbed me. The heads of the various committees stood up to give their verbal and written reports. One pastor I'll call Michael reported on the work his committee had done the previous month.

"But that's not all I have to say," Michael added. "Last night I met with the elders in my church, and a third of them want me to resign. I've never faced such opposition in my life." The man probably talked less than five minutes, but he told of five or six huge problems facing his congregation, one of which was a declining membership. Another was that his daughter was going through a divorce from a physically abusive husband. He added, "I don't know how much more I can handle."

Michael wiped his eyes, obviously holding back from breaking down in front of us. Then he sat down.

No one said a word.

I made no effort to do anything. Instead, I looked around. Among the forty-two people present, I spotted two pastoral counselors and two dozen ordained ministers.

No one said a word.

I stared at our executive, who was busily scratching notes on a piece of paper. One of the professional counselors seemed totally absorbed in his cup of coffee, and the other stared at the ceiling.

No one said a word.

"Let's have the next committee report," the executive said, and he announced the name of the committee. The person got up and presented her report. I couldn't keep my mind on

business. I kept my attention focused on Michael. *Why doesn't
someone say something or go to him? He's hurting. He needs somebody to care.*

We sat at tables that were arranged in a large square, and
Michael sat quite a distance from me. I thought of going over
but then decided that I didn't want to embarrass him or anyone
else by getting up and going across half the room. (I assumed
the others probably felt the same way.) I had no idea what to
say, but that man hurt. We were spiritual leaders, and we made
no attempt to reach out to him.

About twenty minutes later, Michael put his papers in an
attaché case and left. I thought of chasing after him and telling
him how sorry I was about his problems, but I didn't move.

Michael walked out on a Tuesday afternoon. For the next
two days, I kept thinking about him and his situation. His pain
had to be so severe that he couldn't hold back. I was sure he felt
embarrassed. *Somebody needs to reach out to him,* I kept thinking. When I remembered that the executive presbyter had been
writing something, I thought, *He's probably making a note to contact Michael.* I had never talked to Michael except to shake hands
and say hello at business meetings. I was virtually a stranger. *If I
were a friend,* I told myself, *I'd go to him. But he doesn't know me.*
For a few minutes that rationalization satisfied me.

But only for a few minutes. By Thursday evening, I couldn't
shake my concern for Michael. At 8:30 that evening I called him
at home. He answered, and I told him how sad I felt over hearing how badly things were going.

We must have talked for half an hour—or rather Michael
talked. I had no idea how much he was hurting. He struggled
with rejection and problems. Six of his prominent members

threatened to leave. "I just don't know what to do," he said again and again.

I had no wisdom to offer, but I did listen.

Just before I said good-bye, Michael thanked me for calling. "You're the only one," he said.

"What do you mean—'the only one'?"

"All those people in the meeting—and some of them are my golfing buddies—none of them has called. I hardly know you, but you called." He went on to say that he'd never forget my taking time to care.

I didn't confess how hard it had been for me to make the call. I didn't admit that I assumed others would contact him and encourage him. My shock was such that I could only say, "I'm sure many of them care. They probably don't know how to respond."

"So far, you're the only one."

Michael and I talked by phone a few times after that. He told me later that no one else ever called.

Within four months, Michael resigned and accepted a call to a church in Michigan. I heard from him twice after that. Both times he wrote me a short letter. In essence, he said, "When I thought no one cared and that everyone had deserted me, you called." He told me in his first letter that if I had not phoned and encouraged him, he would have left the pastorate in discouragement. He had just finished saying, "God, unless someone reaches out to me, I'm leaving the ministry forever." Then came my phone call.

I played the hero in that story—okay, a reluctant hero—but I learned an invaluable lesson too. For the next few years, until

I resigned to write full time, I made it a point to contact every pastor I heard about who was having problems. I didn't do anything outstanding. I called; I listened. Nothing more.

One church leader called me an "angel of light." To my surprise, most of them volunteered the information that no one else had reached out to them. This statement isn't meant to blame others. It is to say that until Michael broke down in public, I thought little about reaching out to other ministers. After my experience with him, I felt badly that I had been insensitive to hurting clergy and other leaders. My actions certainly weren't on the same level as Onesiphorus going to visit an imprisoned Paul; however, I like to think my efforts served the same sort of purpose.

Paul said that Onesiphorus wasn't ashamed of the apostle's chains. By that, I think he meant that although Paul was in prison, his friend was willing to do whatever he could to reach out to him. The man didn't stay away for fear of being imprisoned himself for being a believer. He did what he could.

God convicted me of my failure to reach out to the hurting ones around me. When I read that wonderful statement about Onesiphorus, I know there's one man who did it right. I admire the commitment and sensitivity of reaching out and of not being concerned about his own convenience. We never hear anything else about Onesiphorus. He probably wasn't a prominent leader, *but he cared.* That's what makes him someone to hold up as a role model. He must have visited Paul in Rome and reached out to him—and reached out when he would have had every excuse not to search for the apostle.

I am Onesiphorus.

Help me not to wait for others to come to me
with their hurts.

I want to care and to reach out to those in pain.

22

ONE ALONE

Standing alone isn't easy.

I wonder how many of us have been in the place where we ask, "Am I the only one?" "Does anyone else care?" And sometimes we go on to ask, "What's wrong with me?"

I was teaching one year in a prestigious writers' conference. The presidential debates started on our final evening, just before two of us began to team-teach a late-night session. About twenty minutes before we finished, a woman walked in, interrupted the class, and enthusiastically announced that she had been listening to the debates.

"Who won?" someone asked.

"Our man did," she replied.

"Who is 'our man'?" I asked, although I had already figured out who she meant.

Several people laughed. "You're not for [_____],
are you?"

"As a matter of fact, that's probably who I'll vote for," I said.

"You have to be kidding," the newcomer said.

"I thought you were a Christian," another said with a chuckle.

By then, I had finished my role for the night, and my teaching partner (who was for "our man") took over the last part of the session. As I sat and listened during the final minutes, I felt totally alone. I may have imagined it, but the opinion seemed to be that if I were a real Christian, I would have joined the parade for "our man."

Although I felt uncomfortable in that situation, it wasn't the first time I'd stood alone. For example, once when I taught public school, I opposed a dozen teachers who wanted to promote a gambling idea at the PTA to raise money. I had expected them to disagree, because I knew mine was distinctly a minority voice. Even when we realize such facts, though, it's difficult, sometimes painful, to be around when those with whom we have much in common—such as faith in Christ—can produce such gaps that we feel we're alone.

Here's one other time I felt absolutely alone—and probably the one that brought me the most pain. Shirley and I had been very active in a small but affluent congregation on the north side of Chicago. We felt God call us to serve in Africa, contacted a mission board, were accepted, and began our preparations to leave the country.

The pastor of our church—someone I loved dearly—called me on the phone. "This is not God's will," he said.

For perhaps ten minutes he lectured me, insisting that God had not called us. He never quite said he didn't believe in sending missionaries to other lands, but he did say that national Christians in that country should be held accountable to evangelize and teach their people without any outside "interference."

No matter how carefully I tried to explain our position, my pastor refuted every statement. Finally he said, "We stand against your god on Mount Carmel."

His words shocked me so much that I couldn't believe he had made such a terrible statement.

"What did you say?"

He repeated the statement.

I hung up—I had to because his words hurt so deeply I couldn't speak. He had broken my heart. That was the congregation for whom Shirley and I had worked and served for four years. One summer I had served as the assistant pastor and oversaw all the summer programs. I loved those people, and I felt that I belonged to them and they to us.

I knew what the pastor meant. He referred to the congregation and him as being Elijah on Mount Carmel opposing me, represented by the 450 prophets of Baal. (First Kings 18:16–46 tells the complete story.)

Nothing so far in my Christian experience had crushed me that deeply. Those were my brothers and sisters—individuals and families I had known and loved. The pastor was someone I had loved as if he were my father.

We felt dazed and confused. We did call one woman. "We've been told not to speak to you," she said, "so I don't feel I can disobey." She hung up.

We felt more isolated than ever. It hurt to be rejected by our own brothers and sisters in Christ. We continued with our plans because we had absolute certainty of God's call.

I share these stories because sometimes faithfulness means standing alone and feeling that not a single soul in the universe feels the same way.

When Elijah boldly spoke up for the Lord on Mount Carmel, believers were presumably among the crowd, although the text never says so. That must have been a painful, discouraging time for Elijah, but it wasn't an isolated event. For three and a half years he had been running from King Ahab and Queen Jezebel. The prophet had told them that it wouldn't rain during all that time—and it didn't—so the king sought to kill him.

Now comes the showdown. Now he stands alone against all the powerful leaders of Samaria, including the king.

After the false prophets are unable to call fire down from heaven to burn their sacrifice, Elijah makes people wet down the sacrifice as well as the wood on which the animal lay. In fact, he made them do it three times, "and the water ran around the altar and even overflowed the trench" (1 Kings 18:35, NLT).

Elijah prays for God to vindicate him. "Immediately the fire of the LORD flashed down from heaven and burned up the young bull, the wood, the stones, and the dust. It even licked up the water in the ditch!" (verse 38).

When the assembly witnessed the miracle, "They fell on their faces and cried out, 'The LORD is God! The LORD is God!'" (verse 39).

Elijah commanded the people to seize the prophets of Baal, and Elijah kills them.

That's not the end of Elijah's standing alone. He prays for rain, and after three and a half years of drought, thundershowers cover the land. Once the rain has returned, the prophet hears that Jezebel had threatened his life. The Bible says, "Elijah was afraid and fled for his life" (1 Kings 19:3, NLT). He and his servant run from Samaria in the north to Beersheba in the south. There the prophet leaves his servant and goes into the desert alone for a full day's journey.

I've never understood why Elijah suddenly becomes so fearful. This was the time of great triumph for him. Hordes of people have now turned to the Lord. Ahab and Jezebel have been after him for years, so this is no new threat.

My assumption is that he was worn out. Today we might call him depressed or simply burned out. He gave himself at Mount Carmel, and he had been running and hiding. He was tired; his resistance and energy were down. After those years of being hunted and haunted, the new threat must have been too much.

Elijah ran away—that's the point. He was not only afraid, but something more powerful drove him. He felt as if he alone stood up for God. That's a terrible feeling.

At one point he felt so depressed that he wanted to die. "Then he went on alone into the desert, traveling all day. He sat down under a solitary broom tree and prayed that he might die. 'I have had enough, LORD,' he said. 'Take my life, for I am no better than my ancestors'" (19:4).

God didn't take his life, but the depression continued. Finally, in his isolation, the prophet cried out, "I have zealously served the LORD God Almighty. But the people of Israel have broken their covenant with you, torn down your altars, and killed every one of your prophets. I alone am left, and now they are trying to kill me, too" (1 Kings 19:10, NLT).

A lengthy passage follows, and we read of the prophet's terrible sense of despair. God speaks to him in a still, small voice (verse 12), but he still feels alone.

God then says something to the prophet—something he badly needs to hear. "Yet I will preserve seven thousand others in Israel who have never bowed to Baal or kissed him!" (verse 18).

What a powerful statement! Elijah finally grasped a powerful truth: he felt alone, but he wasn't alone. Feeling alone,

he learned, isn't always the same as being deserted or without help.

⇒

I chose Elijah as a model because his ordeal makes me think of
things I don't want to face. Yes, he ran. Yes, he was afraid. Even
so, he never turned from God. He moaned and groaned because
he felt isolated and betrayed, but we find no evidence that he
planned to quit.

This story is a quiet rebuke to me. I've sometimes been
silent rather than speaking up. If I speak up, others may disagree. Or sometimes I've salved my conscience by saying, "My
opinion won't matter anyway, and if I keep silent, I won't hurt
anyone's feelings."

Although the outcome is considerably more serious with
the prophet, the story reminds me that speaking up isn't a matter of hurting feelings or not hurting them but of standing
up for what I believe. I wouldn't openly deny Jesus Christ; I
wouldn't hide my commitment if someone asked. However,
I have allowed silence to keep me from making it known that
I'm not aligning myself with the majority opinion.

It reminds me of something a British minister once said.
"When the apostle Paul went to a city, he brought revival and
riot. When I go to a city, they serve me tea." He gently rebuked
a number of us for being what he called "nice, civilized people."
It's the old bit of going along to get along.

I don't want to suggest that we should intentionally offend
or stand up and argue over minor issues. I know I need more of
the vision and the courage of Elijah to stand up for what's right,
honorable, and true.

I haven't always done that, and I've felt guilty for it after-ward. This man's experience encourages me. I've chosen Elijah as my role model to stand for what I believe in, even if others don't agree.

> *I am Elijah.*
> *I love you, God, and I'm prepared to stand up*
> *   for what I believe—even if other believers*
> *   don't agree.*
> *I yearn to hear your voice so strongly that it will*
> *   mute all the other voices.*

23

THE SIGNIFICANCE OF THE INSIGNIFICANT

Most of us like heroes, and we're especially impressed by the Abraham Lincoln kind of man. American children learn that the great president had little formal education, that he often walked miles to borrow a book, and that he was scrupulously honest.

Or I think of the actor Charles Bronson, who died in late 2003. He was one of thirteen children in a coal-mining family. The family was so poor that he once had to wear a hand-me-down dress from his sister in order for him to go to school. Before his death at age eighty-one, he became one of Hollywood's leading actors.

Ben Carson lived in Detroit's inner city and was virtually illiterate in the fifth grade. That's when his mother learned that he was falling behind in school and insisted that he read two books a week and write a report on each one. Within a year, he was one of the best readers in his class. By the time he finished high school, Ben won a scholarship to Yale.[10]

---

10. See Ben Carson with Cecil Murphey, Gifted Hands (Grand Rapids, MI: Zondervan, 1990).

These are people who would otherwise have been ignored or overlooked. They are ostensibly the insignificant individuals in this world, and yet they overcame the odds. I point to outstanding people like these three because they break the rules. They rise above what anyone would expect of them.

In the Bible, Gideon was a person who had just about everything going against him. For one thing, he was illegitimate—that carried a heavy social stigma in those days.

This was a man whose family lived in fear, hiding their crops from the enemy. One day, however, God sends an angel to break into Gideon's world. He finds the farmer threshing wheat in the hidden field and commands him to save Israel from the Midianites. The man's first argument is that if God is with the Israelites, why is an enemy overpowering the country? It's an excuse that says, in effect, "Why me?" Instead of answering the question, the messenger tells the farmer that God will give him strength to save Israel.

An incredulous Gideon can't take in that he's to be the savior of the nation. "My clan is the weakest in Manasseh, and I am the least in my family" (Judges 6:15, NIV). The word translated "weak" in Hebrew is *dal* and it means "lowly"—that is, insignificant. Gideon also points out that he's the youngest in the family—the lowest position.

The angel answers, "The LORD is with you, mighty warrior" (verse 12). The word written "LORD" (large capital L and small capitals for the rest) is the way translators write the sacred name of Yahweh (or Jehovah). This is more than just to say, "God is going to be with you." It's like saying, "Yahweh—the great I AM—will empower you."

Gideon starts his work for God hesitantly and fearfully. "Because he was afraid of his family and the men in the town, he did it at night rather than in the daytime" (verse 27). In the dead of night he tears down his own father's altar to Baal and builds a proper altar. He burns the pole that honored a pagan god and uses the wood to burn a sacrifice to the true God. At first the people are angry—until they realize that Gideon has dared to take such drastic action because God has given him a mission. Others join Gideon to stand up against their enemy.

Of course, Gideon still has problems believing he is worthy of God's calling. There follows the famous fleece story. Gideon cries out to God and says, in effect, "If you have called me, here's how you can show me. Tonight I'm going to put a piece of fleece on the threshing floor. In the morning, if there is dew only on the wool and not on the floor, I'll believe." God answers that request: in the morning, only the fleece is wet.

Still not convinced, Gideon reverses the request by asking God to keep the wool dry but to make the floor wet. That's exactly what God does.

Like many of us, Gideon still has trouble believing that God has favored and called him. He rounds up those who want to fight, gets rid of all but three hundred—as God instructed—and still isn't sure he's capable of doing what God wants accomplished. Once again, God graciously responds.

Gideon and one of his servants creep up on one of the camps of the Midianites. At the moment they arrive, one of the guards tells the other about a dream in which Gideon and his people defeat them.

Finally assured of God's empowerment, Gideon and his soldiers go into battle, defeat the Midianites, and celebrate their victory. Instead of despising him, now the Israelites urge him to become their king. But he says, "I will not rule over you, nor will my son rule over you. The LORD will rule over you" (8:23).

I can easily identify with Gideon. He's the man who just can't believe God has called him to accomplish any great feats. It's as if he says, "Who am I? There are so many others who are better qualified." This is the underdog, the insignificant, the person who has no special talent.

However, he's the person God points to and says, "I want you. I will raise you up, and I'll show my power through you." I've marveled over the fact that God allowed Gideon only three hundred soldiers. When the Israelites were ready to fight, they had thirty-two thousand soldiers ready for battle. But God said, "You have too many men for me to deliver Midian into their hands. In order that Israel may not boast against me that her own strength has saved her, announce now to the people, 'Anyone who trembles with fear may turn back and leave Mount Gilead'" (7:2, 3).

Gideon now has ten thousand left.

Still too many, God says.

When Gideon narrows the number down again, God says, "With the three hundred men . . . I will save you and give the Midianites into your hands" (verse 7). With that small force, God saves the nation under the leadership of Gideon.

Who was this man? A nobody. A farmer. A fearful Israelite. But he's the person God chose. For me, the Gideon story is more than one about the divine hand on the insignificant. Rather, it's one about a person's struggle to believe that God has chosen him.

"Who, me?" seems to be the question. And Gideon quickly asserts his own unworthiness.

I've felt like Gideon many times—and my struggles don't involve something like saving the United States from our enemies. My doubts and insecurities center on much smaller things.

Take my work as a writer. This book will be book number ninety-one that I've written, cowritten, or ghostwritten. Each time I get in the middle of a project, I find myself wondering how I can ever do an adequate job. *Why did I take this on? I can never produce anything worth reading.* In my case, each time it gets worse instead of easier.

A couple of years ago I wrote a book for a publisher. As I worked on the book, I kept thinking, *This is awful. Terrible. They'll demand that I return the advance and ask me to burn the manuscript.* No matter how hard and how long I worked on the manuscript, I truly felt that way. Finally I turned it in, and the editor wrote back three words: "I like it."

Although I was delighted that he did, I felt inadequate. I still do. I could wail about my impoverished background and my alcoholic father, and of course those *were* factors in my impaired sense of self-worth. The point is that I struggle with feelings of insecurity.

God has called me to write—and that's something totally clear to me. I have no sense that I'm a good writer, an excellent writer, or merely an acceptable one. Each time I send a manuscript to a publisher, I expect it to be thrown back at me. So far it hasn't happened, but every time, I think, *This is the one that will be snickered about at lunch breaks at the publishing house.*

Although I think it's important to know our limitations, it's more important to acknowledge God's nonlimitations. If the great I AM is with us, nothing is impossible and we can do wonderful and exciting things.

Gideon didn't do great things because he believed in his ability. He did great things because he finally believed in the ability of God. That's the yearning I feel: I want to do what God calls me to do. If God calls me, then like Gideon, I will be empowered. And it doesn't matter if the call turns out to be similar to that of a great leader like Lincoln, a famous actor like Bronson, or an internationally recognized surgeon like Dr. Carson.

What matters is that—despite any feelings of insignificance—I listen for God's voice.

> *I am Gideon.*
> *At times I feel insignificant, but you are the significant one.*
> *I am worthy because you have made me worthy.*
> *With your help, I am able to do every task you set before me.*

24

THE QUIET LISTENER

Almost anyone who has been in the church for a period of time knows the story. Luke tells it in five verses (Luke 10:38–42). Mary and Martha are sisters and, as we learn from John's Gospel, Lazarus is their brother. In this incident Jesus visits their home.

Martha flutters around getting things ready while Mary sits at Jesus' feet. Finally, a frustrated Martha scolds Jesus. "Lord, don't you care that my sister has left me to do the work by myself? Tell her to help me!" (verse 40, NIV).

First, I think Martha gets a bum rap. By that I mean she gets labeled as doing something wrong and is always looked down upon because of it.

Mary did choose the better part—when Jesus was there. But what was she like when Jesus wasn't visiting? Mary makes me think of a man named Dick who came to Kenya as a missionary only months before I returned to the United States. He was a man of prayer. In fact, he was a man of much prayer—so much and so protracted that he accomplished little actual work. Whatever tasks came up, Dick smiled and said, "I've decided to set the day aside for prayer and fasting."

I don't intend to deride the man, and I believe he was sincere. I'm sure he prayed and fasted as he said he would. His coworkers told me Dick prayed as much as four or five hours every day—but he didn't get much work done. In fact, the others who labored with him had to take over part of his load. He was a part-time worker and a full-time pray-er.

That's not even slightly close to who I am. I'm the activist—like Martha. I like to *do*. It's hard for me to sit quietly. When I was a child, I was such a wiggler that my mother once said, "You can't sit still for five minutes." Later that day I got out the clock and decided to prove I could. It wasn't easy, but I did sit without moving for an entire five minutes.

Even when I sit in church, I'm moving my toes or shifting positions. That's part of who I am. I have difficulty praying on my knees for any extended period of time. I do my best praying at 5:00 in the morning as I run through the darkened streets in my neighborhood. As long as my body moves, my mind stays focused on spiritual things.

That's a picture of the kind of person I am. I fidget constantly. Even when nothing else moves, I'm sometimes aware that I'm wiggling my toes. All of that is to show that I'm an official, certified activist.

I'm Martha, and I like being Martha; I also yearn to be Mary.

I admire people who can sit and pray and read and spend hours every day with Jesus. Too often, however, we're presented with that type of individual as the ideal picture of Christian commitment. I think it's not only a wrong portrait of Martha, but also a wrong one of Mary.

As I've thought of this story, it seems to me that we have to read it in context. The problem doesn't seem to be one of day-to-day living, but only an issue of what to do when Jesus comes. Mary is ready to put away her work and listen; Martha hurries and worries, always trying to fix things up and having a lot on her mind.

If we put this into modern terms, I suspect most of us are like Martha. We find it difficult to push aside our worries, problems, and concerns. Even if we set aside time for prayer, events around us sometimes distract our thinking. We try to read the Bible, and we think of twelve things we need to do that day or the next. It's not easy to push those concerns aside, and it takes discipline to overcome those disturbing thoughts.

What I like about Mary, however, is that when "Jesus time" approaches, she is able to leave everything and focus on her guest. She pushes aside the worries and concerns that must trouble her as much as her sister.

I think of the sisters as representing the activist and the contemplative. Perhaps this is exaggerated, but it helps me make my point.

As I've said, by nature, I'm very much of the Martha style. My wife, however, is like Mary. I'm not aware of a day when she hasn't had a special set-aside time to be with Jesus. It seems easy and natural for her.

I admire my wife and the other Marys of the world. I wish I were more contemplative. I can say that I'm learning to be slightly less of an activist. I've disciplined myself to read in long snatches, sometimes three hours with no more than a toilet break. It's not natural for me and constantly challenges me.

Instead of choosing one style over the other, however, I've sought to adapt to both of them. I yearn to be quieter and to have a deeper "Jesus time." I also like being on the move.

Isn't it possible to combine the best of both sisters? I think it is. Here's how I see this middle ground. When I'm up and active, I want to be fully engaged in what I do. One of my friends calls this mindfulness—being totally aware of my actions and even my thoughts.

Because I'm easily a Martha and that takes no particular energy from me, I've chosen to focus on Mary. I don't want to become like Dick, who fits the stereotype of being so heavenly minded that he's no earthly good.

I yearn to be Mary, who hears the voice of Jesus that calls to her to "Come apart and rest awhile." I want to be Mary, who is content to leave pots and pans and schedules and chores and phone calls and e-mail messages, and focus on Jesus Christ.

I yearn to develop the contemplative part of my life and to be more open to the quietness and lack of activity around me. I want to be like Mary.

I am Mary.
Help me to sit each day at your feet—and listen
*   and learn.*
I am Mary; help me grow quieter in your
*   presence.*

25

THE WORLD'S MOST HUMBLE

● ● ● and, Lord, keep us humble. Amen."

I had been a Christian only a few months, and it was one of the first midweek prayer meetings I had ever attended. The man's words shocked me.

Keep us humble? I asked myself silently. *Doesn't that imply that we're already humble?* Then I almost laughed out loud as I thought, *Only the truly nonhumble would pray that way.*

A few years ago I was teaching at a conference in New Mexico and a woman rushed up to me, introduced herself, and rattled off the names of several mutual friends. We chatted a few minutes and she said, "You're exactly the way they said you were. You're so humble."

I smiled outwardly, but inwardly I bristled. I had no idea what she meant. Was I obsequious? I didn't think so. Did I fawn over her? No, I didn't. What did she mean? I wasn't sure. From the way she talked, I was sure she meant it as a compliment, but I wasn't certain it was a label I wanted to wear.

Obviously, I didn't have a good handle on the word *humble*—and I don't think most people do either. I'd read Numbers

12:3 for years in the King James Version: "Now the man Moses was very meek, above all the men which were upon the face of the earth."

Meek or humble? In most minds, either word carries the idea of being spineless and weak. It's the same word Jesus uses in the Beatitudes where he promises a blessing for the meek. In Greek, it's *praus*. It was a word used in connection with animals—those that had been trained to obey the commands of their human leader. They submitted to the reins of the owner. It also refers to animals that had learned to accept control by their owner. The implication is that it's not a natural attribute but a quality gained only from experience—hard experience.

This isn't so much a matter of being self-controlled, for who of us truly is? It's a way of looking to those who are God-controlled. When Jesus pronounces a blessing on the meek, he must surely refer to those who submit to and remain under God's control—those who have learned to obey God in every way.

With that kind of meaning attached to being meek or humble, I'm all for it.

Recently, however, I was reading the same verse in a modern version. "Now Moses was more humble than any other person on earth" (NLT).

I brushed up on my rusty biblical languages and looked up that word "humble." Moses doesn't come across to me as humble. When God first called him, he gave a lot of excuses, saying he wasn't eloquent. So God said Aaron would be his speaker.

Nothing else in the accounts shows a mild-mannered, retiring soul (as I assumed "humble" or "meek" meant). Moses constantly defied the king of Egypt. After the Hebrews went into the wilderness, Moses frequently stood alone against an entire nation that wished to return to Egyptian captivity. One man against a million or more sounds like anything but a mild, retiring person. He roused the people to battle against Amalek's attack. Yet he never hesitated to mete out punishment to those disobeying divine commands.

Moses showed deep anger by forcing the people to drink the bits of gold they had once used to build the idol of the golden calf. He stood against the enemies of the nation and the enemies within the nation.

This is the same man to whom God gave the offer to wipe out the nation and start over again with him. He prayed, "Yet now if you will only forgive their sin—and if not, then blot *me* out of the book you have written" (Exodus 32:32, TLB).

That's humility in action. This is the man of whom God said he was the meekest (most humble) on earth.

Besides Moses, Jesus presents another example of humility. His words, recorded in Matthew 11:29, read, "Take my yoke upon you. Let me teach you, because I am humble and gentle, and you will find rest for your souls. For my yoke fits perfectly, and the burden I give you is light" (NLT).

This is a far different picture from those of Jesus I see displayed in some Sunday school classrooms. In the New Testament we read of the man who chased money changers from the Temple with a whip. He publicly rebuked religious leaders. One time he denounced Peter as a tool of Satan. He fearlessly went to death on a cross after refusing to bow down or defend himself before false accusers. This is the biblical picture of humility. The humble are those who submit themselves to God.

The humble stand in the face of opposition, but they don't lash out in blind anger. They don't retaliate for unkind deeds.

Instead, they submit themselves to God's will, regardless of what it is or where God sends them.

If we continue to think of humility as I did in the beginning, that's not a quality any of us would yearn for. But if we see this quality in a positive light, as referring to obedience and commitment, we can change our thinking.

I yearn to be truly humble (in the biblical sense of the word), but I'm still uncomfortable about the term. I can applaud Moses and worship Jesus—the truly humble. When it comes to myself, I struggle.

Perhaps this story will help. A few years ago, several friends joined a particular church that was known for its outreach and discipleship program. Within weeks after they joined, I noticed that they inserted a statement in their conversation that bothered me. "I'm fully committed to God."

Worse than bothering me, their words repelled me. "I want to be fully committed," I finally said to one of them, "but if I have to tell someone, doesn't that imply something is wrong with me? Isn't it better to live the life and let others say it?"

"This is our testimony. We're not trying to be boastful," she said; "we're trying to be honest."

Maybe she was right.

Even if others say it to me, as I mentioned above, I'm still extremely uncomfortable. I finally figured out the reason. I want to live as totally committed to God as I can. The problem is, I live inside my skin and know my shortcomings, failures, and weaknesses. I know how often I struggle. As soon as I use words about myself such as "total commitment," a voice inside begins to laugh, as if to say, *Who do you think you're trying to deceive?*

So here's my secret: I yearn to be humble. I hesitate to say the words, and yet I've learned something else about praying this way. The more I pray a prayer such as "I am Moses, and I am humble," the more I crawl in that direction. Perhaps "crawl" is too strong a word; maybe I only gently scoot that way. But right now it's not the destination I'm concerned about, but the journey.

I want nothing to hinder my relationship with the Savior. I want be able to say, "I am Moses, and I am humble." Of all the prayers in this book that I've shared with you, this is the one I still have the most trouble with. Yes, admittedly, part of it is probably my own hang-up over words such as *humble, meek,* or *committed.* So here's how I handle this. I am praying this prayer, but it's not one I can easily talk about. I live with the sense that if I say such words, I'll be speaking in pride.

This is difficult to write because (I assume) many people will read these words. My only source of peace is to keep telling myself—as I do with the other prayers in this book—this may not be true yet, but one day it will be a reality. I'm creeping slowly in that direction.

> *I am Moses.*
> *I am humble, because I am obedient.*
> *Help me be as fully committed to you as I know*
> *   how to be.*

26

WANTING MORE

Accord to the way some students count miracles, Elisha performed exactly twice as many as Elijah. That, they explain, answers his prayer for a double portion of Elijah's spirit (2 Kings 2:9). Maybe twice as many miracles satisfy most people as the proper explanation, but I can't believe that satisfied Elisha.

The first time we read of Elisha is in 1 Kings 19, where it says that Elijah found the younger man plowing his field and called him. "Elijah went up to him and threw his cloak around him" (verse 19, NIV). Elisha understands the meaning of that gesture: He will receive the prophet's mantle. That is, he will become Elijah's successor. The protégé asks permission to set his affairs in order, which Elijah grants, and the chapter ends with these words: "Then he set out to follow Elijah and became his attendant" (verse 21).

The succession is recorded in 2 Kings 2. Elijah tells his protégé that if he wants to succeed him, the learner must stay with the master. One day the two men are on their way to Gilgal, and Elijah says, "Stay here; the LORD has sent me to Bethel" (verse 2).

"But Elisha said, 'As surely as the LORD lives and as you live, I will not leave you.'" This shows us the commitment of the disciple.

There seems to be a bit of odd zigzagging after this. They start at Gilgal near the Jordan River and go to Bethel, which is about four thousand feet higher and fifteen miles away. Then they go to Jericho, located near Gilgal, and finally move toward the Jordan. I see in these marches the continuing drama of Elijah putting his disciple to the test. They seem also to be retracing (in reverse) some of Israel's first steps into the Promised Land (Joshua 5–8) before they reenact the earlier wonderful crossing of the Jordan (Joshua 3–4).

The parting scene is straightforward. Just before Elijah goes up to heaven in a whirlwind, he asks a question: "Tell me, what can I do for you before I am taken from you?"

"'Let me inherit a double portion of your spirit,' Elisha replied" (2 Kings 2:9, NIV). The double share of Elijah's spirit suggests the portion given to the older son or heir.

This time the older prophet, who seems to have attempted to dissuade Elisha, sets as a condition that he must be present to see when his master is taken. To "see," of course, isn't only to observe, but rather it also carries the idea of understanding.

Elisha watches as a chariot of fire comes from heaven and carries Elijah upward. He cries out, "My father! My father!" (verse 12), which further emphasizes the idea of the father-son relationship.

As soon as Elijah is gone, Elisha picks up the cloak that his mentor had dropped. As an act of his unworthiness, he ritually tears his own clothes. He has fulfilled the condition—he has seen and he inherits. Elisha takes the mantle and strikes the water with it, and the waters part—the reverse of the original crossing of Jordan.

"When the group of prophets from Jericho saw what happened, they exclaimed, 'Elisha has become Elijah's successor!'" (verse 15, NLT).

As I've thought about that event, I've always been impressed by Elisha's request for a double portion of the older man's spirit. It's not a greedy act in which he's saying, "You're good, and God uses you. I want twice as much fame and power as you have."

Instead, I see this as a cry for more of God in his life. I suspect it may also be a reflective statement. By that I mean, what if Elisha views himself as inadequate, unworthy, and ungifted? He then asks for a double portion just to come up to the same level as his mentor.

Regardless of what may be the best interpretation to put on the story, Elisha stands out as my role model. This is the man I want to imitate. This is where I find myself crying out, "God, give me more." I have no idea what I mean when I ask God for more. Is it possible that Elisha didn't either? When we cry out like that, aren't we speaking of our yearning for a greater awareness or a deeper commitment?

When I think of Elisha's yearning, it nearly always throws me back to Jesus' words of blessing in the Sermon on the Mount:

> Blessed are those who hunger and thirst for righteous-
> ness, for they will be filled. (Matthew 5:6, NIV)

I like to think that, instead of the prophet's request being unusual, his was a normal request for any of God's people. We come into the faith at some point in our lives and begin to follow the Spirit's guidance. We rejoice in the good things going on. And if we feed ourselves through the Bible—praying, teaching and preaching, and being with other believers—that hunger intensifies. Obviously, at some points it's more pronounced than at others, but this is the normal progress of the Christian experience.

God's intention for us is to yearn for more.

To cry out and say, "Bless me with more of you in my life," is not only the right thing, but isn't it—shouldn't it be—the normal Christian life? Perhaps the trouble is that too many believers are satisfied with less. As a friend once said to me, "I know I'll be inside heaven's gates when the end comes. That's enough for me."

I also realize that we have varying spiritual capacities. Some seem content with little, while others never reach a place of spiritual satisfaction. For the second group, there is always the longing for more. Maybe it's because they've tasted enough of intimacy with God that it makes them aware of how little they actually have.

I don't know about others; I do know about myself. I want more of God. I yearn for more. It's a matter of almost daily prayer for me.

At the same time, my understanding of the Bible says that the hunger I have came from God. Perhaps all Christians don't have that burning desire for more. Or at least they *seem* not to crave it. It's not my responsibility to compare myself with them or to decide on their level and compare it with mine. My task is to open myself to God.

In writing the paragraphs above, I cringe because the words may sound as if I perceive myself as living on some sort of super-spiritual level far above others. That isn't true. I have no idea where I stand in relation to other Christians—and it's not something I think about. I want to walk as far up the mountain as the Spirit will take me.

When I was young in the faith (I became a believer in my early twenties), I used to hear church people talk about "babes in Christ," the "immature," and sometimes "carnal believers." Of course, they always spoke as those who considered themselves mature.

I also remember that I talked with a group of older Christians (older in every way) and tried to explain my burning hunger for more of God. Because each of them had been in the faith for at least fifty years, I thought they would guide me.

"You'll calm down," one of them said. He implied that I'd become "normal" and lose my zealous yearning.

And at times in my life, the hunger has been more latent than active. I do know that I truly want whatever God has for me—and I want all of it.

One of the most significant lessons I've learned about my own spiritual growth shocked me and confused me for a long time. I went through a period of a couple of years during which I kept asking God to enrich my life, to draw me close, to make me more like Jesus Christ.

What I discovered is that I kept seeing obstacles in my pathway. I became aware of harsh words that I hadn't perceived as mean or unkind. Small, thoughtless, and petty actions hounded me. I seemed to eat large portions of guilt every day. I felt as if the more I yearned for God, the more I failed.

At times I'm a slow learner, but I finally figured out that having more of God doesn't mean living a life of continuous victory and skipping from one mountaintop experience to another. When God begins to satisfy that yearning, we go inward. We examine our motives. We look at the little things about ourselves that we hadn't noticed before. Our attitudes cause us to bow our heads in shame. Perhaps that should have been obvious to me; it took me a long time to figure out.

A few years ago, I was working with an extremely talented writer named Mike Brewer, and he was part of a group of six people who met regularly. I was harder on Mike than I was on the others. Although he had published articles, children's pieces, and devotionals, I saw immense talent in him and wanted him to move into writing books and to challenge himself more. Mike always took the criticism well, but one day when we had lunch together, he said something to the effect that I was tough on him.

"I am. I'm tougher, harder, and meaner to you than I am to the others. You're farther down the road than they are, but that's not the reason. It's because you have greater potential. I refuse to let you settle for being less than you can be."

As of this writing, Mike has finished his second contracted book, and he's going to do well. He has the divinely bestowed talent to go far.

By contrast, I worked with another writer whose first name was Rick. He had great talent, but it wasn't developed. He could play several instruments, was an able carpenter, and could deliver an interesting sermon. In fact, I don't know anything that Rick couldn't do well. He never excelled at anything—but he was always good.

Rick met me at a writers' conference and begged me to mentor him. I agreed and worked with him to develop his writing skills, but he dropped out after a few months. "I'm just too busy," he said. When I pushed him, Rick admitted that writing was just too much work, and he wasn't prepared to throw himself into it.

Isn't that how the Christian life works? The more we put in, the more we receive. But there's also the fact that we have to see our shortcomings and failures before we can overcome them and move on. Okay, that *sounds* simple, but that's still the principle of spiritual growth.

I'm still trudging up the mountain path. Some days I look up and think I'm getting nowhere. Or I feel as the Israelites did when they kept going around and around getting nowhere. After forty years of wandering, Moses reports, "When we were at Mount Sinai, the LORD our God said to us, 'You have stayed at this mountain long enough. It is time to break camp and move on'" (Deuteronomy 1:6, 7, NLT). God directed them and added, "I am giving all this land to you! Go in and occupy it" (verse 8).

That's the promise—go in and occupy. Move forward. Like Elisha, I want everything God will give me.

The truth is, I tend to be hard on myself. And I assume most of us are. I think of all the things I know about living the Christian life, and then I fail to live up to what I know. I pause to look downward. I remember the valley I was living in before I started my upward trek. I remember my lapses and shortcomings, but I think God is saying—as Paul did about himself to the Philippians (see Philippians 3:13, 14)—"Forget that which is behind. Press onward. Go forward."

I'm not anywhere near the top, but each day I move a few steps closer. I think that's how the yearning process works. If we ask for more—whether it's a double portion or just a gnawing hunger—it's not easy growth, and it's not instant or automatic.

But I know God is with us and that our requests for "more" please him, even if we're not sure what we mean.

> *I am Elisha.*
> *I want more, even though I'm not sure what I'm*
>   *asking for.*
> *God, I want more of your control in my life.*

A FINAL WORD

W hy did I choose this method of prayer? This way to search for more of God in my life? My first response is pragmatic: because it works for me.

Only in writing this book have I realized another reason. Some of us (I really mean me) aren't readily introspective. We don't easily search inward and examine our motives. Disappointments, rejections, or tragic events often have to crash into our lives to push us toward deeper introspection. In my case, no tragedies occurred. I simply felt a need in my life for a more vigorous relationship with God.

It was like having a thirst that nothing quenches. I wanted more—no, I had to have more.

As the yearning grew, I often had no idea how to go about satisfying it. Where do I start? What disciplines do I need? How do I know I'm moving in the right direction? After all, I'd been a Christian for many years, and I knew all the traditional methods.

"Give me more," I prayed daily for weeks.

Then something happened. I realized that often—although not every day—I'd read a verse or a story in my Bible that wouldn't let me go. No matter how many times I'd read the section previously, it felt as if the message was new. I paused and pondered those. I'd done that before, but this time it was different. Not only was the pause longer, but in addition I realized that I kept thinking about the words for days at a time.

I started this book by referring to Romans 9:13: "Jacob I loved." My mind returned to that verse several times each day for weeks. Unable to push Romans 9:13 out of my mind, I began to think of myself as Jacob and relishing the certainty of God's loving me.

The more I began to focus on Jacob, the more I found myself understanding the verse and applying it to my life.

That's how this started. I called it my experiment with prayer. The other chapters also evolved out of reading passages from the Bible that didn't seem to want me to move on. I decided that whenever I read anything that touched me deeply in the Bible— negatively or positively—I would accept that as the Holy Spirit speaking to me. That meant my willingness to spend time reflecting on specific passages and praying for God's help in applying them to me personally.

I've been using this style of prayer for about four years. I figured out that it was easier for me to go inward by seeing myself in others or seeing what I yearned to be. That's easier than to take an exploration inward without some kind of guidelines or help.

These people from the Bible speak to me. I see myself reflected in them—that is, I see what I want for myself reflected in them. When I think of them, they show me the best parts of living the Christian life. They illustrate for me the commitment I yearn for.

Finally, I came to the conclusion that any method that brought me closer to God was valid and worthwhile. I continued to see new things about myself in reading the Bible—as if God holds up a mirror and says, "You like Elisha, do you? You can become like him."

I continue to yearn for more.

I am still learning.
Teach me, God—teach me to pray and to live so
that every part of my life honors you.